Dream New York: A Travel Preparation Guide.

Daniel Hunter

All rights reserved. No part of this publication may be reproduced, distributed, or transmitted in any form or by any means, including photocopying, recording, or other electronic or mechanical methods, without the prior written permission of the publisher, except in the case of brief quotations embodied in critical reviews and certain other noncommercial uses permitted by copyright law.

Copyright © (Daniel Hunter) (2023).

TABLE OF CONTENTS

Chapter 1. Introduction — 7
- 1.1 Welcome to New York — 7
- 1.2 Getting the Most Out of Your Trip — 8
- 1.3 Travel Tips and Resources — 11

Chapter 2. Planning Your Trip — 15
- 2.1 Choosing the Right Time to Visit — 15
- 2.2 Creating Your Itinerary — 17
- 2.3 Budgeting and Expenses — 21
- 2.4 Accommodation Options — 24
- 2.5 Transportation in the City — 27

Chapter 3. New York City Overview — 31
- 3.1 Geographical Layout — 31
- 3.2 Neighborhoods and Boroughs — 33
- 3.3 Weather and Climate — 36

Chapter 4. Solo Travelers — 39
- 4.1 Safety Tips — 39
- 4.2 Solo-Friendly Activities — 42
- 4.3 Dining Alone — 45
- 4.4 Meeting Locals and Fellow Travelers — 48

Chapter 5. Traveling with Kids — 51
- 5.1 Family-Friendly Attractions — 51
- 5.2 Kid-Friendly Dining — 54
- 5.3 Practical Tips for Parents — 57

Chapter 6. Couples' Getaway — 61
- 6.1 Romantic Spots — 61

6.2 Dining and Date Night Ideas	64
6.3 Planning a Memorable Proposal	67

Chapter 7. Must-See Attractions — 71

7.1 Iconic Landmarks	71
7.2 Museums and Art Galleries	74
7.3 Parks and Outdoor Activities	77
7.4 Entertainment and Broadway Shows	79

Chapter 8. Cultural Experiences — 83

8.1 Art and Theater Scene	83
8.2 Music and Live Performances	86
8.3 Festivals and Events	89
8.4 Historical Sites and Landmarks	92

Chapter 9. Shopping in NYC — 97

9.1 High-End Boutiques	97
9.2 Thrift Stores and Markets	100
9.3 Souvenirs and Unique Finds	103

Chapter 10. Dining and Culinary Delights — 107

10.1 Iconic NYC Foods	107
10.2 Michelin-Star Restaurants	109
10.3 Budget-Friendly Eateries	112
10.4 Dietary Restrictions and Preferences	115

Chapter 11. Nightlife and Entertainment — 119

11.1 Bars and Clubs	119
11.2 Live Music Venues	122
11.3 Comedy Clubs and Theaters	125

Chapter 12. Outdoor Adventures — 129

12.1 Central Park Activities	129
12.2 Biking and Hiking Trails	132
12.3 Waterfront Activities	135

Chapter 13. Practical Information   **139**
   13.1 Local Transportation   139
   13.2 Currency and Banking   141
   13.3 Language and Communication   144
   13.4 Health and Safety   147

Chapter 14. Day Trips and Nearby Attractions 151
   14.1 Exploring Beyond NYC   151

Chapter 15. Traveling with Pets   **155**
   15.1 Pet-Friendly Accommodations   155
   15.2 Dog Parks and Pet Services   158
   15.3 Tips for Traveling with Pets   161

Chapter 16. Resources and Contacts   **165**
   16.1 Tourist Information Centers   165
   16.2 Useful Websites and Apps   168

Chapter 17. Itinerary Ideas   **173**
   17.1 One Week in NYC   173
   17.2 Weekend Getaway Itinerary   175
   17.3 Family-Friendly Itinerary   179
   17.4 Romantic Couples' Itinerary   183

The Tale of the Starry Skyline   **187**

Chapter 1. Introduction

1.1 Welcome to New York

Welcome to the city that never sleeps, the Big Apple, and a destination that truly needs no introduction – New York City. From the towering skyscrapers of Manhattan to the vibrant neighborhoods of Brooklyn, the cultural melting pot of Queens, the rich history of the Bronx, and the scenic beauty of Staten Island, New York City is a place where dreams are made and memories are forged.

In this comprehensive travel guide, we invite you to explore the heart and soul of one of the world's most iconic cities. Whether you're a solo traveler seeking adventure, a family with young explorers, or a couple in search of romance, New York City offers a world of experiences tailored to your preferences.

With its unparalleled blend of history, culture, art, entertainment, and culinary delights, NYC has something for everyone. Wander through the bustling streets, discover hidden gems, and immerse yourself in the electric energy that defines this metropolis.

Our guide will help you navigate the city's neighborhoods, plan your itinerary, find the best dining spots, uncover unique shopping destinations, and tap into the local secrets that make New York City more than just a destination—it's an experience.

So, fasten your seatbelts and get ready to embark on an unforgettable journey through the five boroughs of New York City. Whether you're here for a few days or a longer stay, this guide will be your trusted companion, ensuring that your visit to the Big Apple is filled with adventure, inspiration, and the essence of New York itself. Welcome to the adventure of a lifetime. Welcome to New York City!

1.2 Getting the Most Out of Your Trip

New York City is a bustling metropolis that offers a rich tapestry of experiences for every traveler. To truly savor the essence of this remarkable city, it's essential to plan your visit wisely and make the most of your time in the Big Apple. Here are some tips to ensure you get the most out of your trip to New York:

1. Plan Ahead: The key to a successful New York adventure is planning. Research the city's neighborhoods, attractions, and events in advance.

Create a flexible itinerary that highlights your must-see places while allowing room for spontaneity.

2. Explore Diverse Neighborhoods: New York City is a collection of unique neighborhoods, each with its own character and charm. Venture beyond the tourist hotspots and explore areas like Williamsburg in Brooklyn, the historic streets of Greenwich Village, or the artsy scene in the Lower East Side.

3. Embrace Local Cuisine: NYC is a culinary paradise with a diverse range of dining options. Don't miss the chance to savor iconic New York foods like pizza, bagels, and street vendor hot dogs. Explore the culinary scene further by trying international cuisines from around the world.

4. Take Advantage of Public Transportation: The subway system is the lifeblood of the city, offering an efficient and affordable way to get around. Purchase a MetroCard and hop on the subway to navigate the city like a true New Yorker. You can also use buses and taxis for convenience.

5. Time Your Visits: Many of New York's top attractions can get crowded. To beat the crowds,

consider visiting popular spots early in the morning or during weekdays. You'll have a more enjoyable experience and better photo opportunities.

6. Attend Cultural Events: Check out the city's cultural calendar for concerts, theater productions, art exhibitions, and festivals. New York City's cultural scene is constantly buzzing with world-class performances and events.

7. Enjoy the Parks: Take a break from the urban hustle and relax in one of NYC's beautiful parks. Central Park, Prospect Park, and the High Line offer serene green spaces amidst the city's skyscrapers.

8. Connect with Locals: Strike up conversations with locals, whether it's at a coffee shop, museum, or park. New Yorkers are known for their friendliness and can provide valuable insights and recommendations.

9. Explore Beyond Manhattan: While Manhattan is the heart of NYC, don't forget to explore the other boroughs. Brooklyn, Queens, the Bronx, and Staten Island each have their own hidden gems and unique cultural experiences.

10. Capture Memories: New York City is a photographer's dream. Capture the breathtaking skyline, historic landmarks, and the vibrant street life. Be sure to bring your camera or smartphone to create lasting memories.

Remember that New York City has something for everyone, whether you're interested in art, history, food, or simply absorbing the city's energy. By planning wisely and embracing the diversity of experiences, you'll leave New York with a deep appreciation for this remarkable city.

1.3 Travel Tips and Resources

New York City, often referred to as "The Big Apple," is a bustling metropolis that offers a wealth of experiences for travelers of all kinds. To ensure that your trip to this iconic destination is as smooth and enjoyable as possible, here are some essential travel tips and resources to keep in mind:

1. Planning Your Trip:
   - Timing Is Key: New York experiences four distinct seasons, each with its own charm. Consider your preferences for weather and crowds when choosing the time to visit.
   - Book Early: Popular attractions, accommodations, and Broadway shows can sell out

quickly. Make reservations in advance to secure your spot.
   - Itinerary Planning: Create a flexible itinerary that includes must-see attractions but leaves room for spontaneity.

2. Budgeting and Expenses:
   - Daily Costs: NYC can be expensive, so plan your budget accordingly. Be mindful of expenses like accommodation, dining, transportation, and entertainment.
   - Discount Passes: Consider purchasing attraction passes like the CityPASS or Explorer Pass to save money on admission fees.
   - Tipping: Tipping is customary in the United States. Be prepared to tip service staff at restaurants, hotels, and taxis.

3. Accommodation Options:
   - Diverse Choices: New York City offers a wide range of accommodation options, from luxury hotels to budget-friendly hostels and vacation rentals.
   - Location Matters: Choose accommodations in proximity to your planned activities to save time and transportation costs.

4. Transportation in the City:

- Subway System: NYC's subway system is the most convenient and affordable way to get around. Purchase a MetroCard for easy access.
- Taxi and Ride-Sharing: Taxis and ride-sharing services like Uber and Lyft are readily available but can be more expensive than public transit.
- Walking: NYC is a pedestrian-friendly city, so bring comfortable walking shoes and explore neighborhoods on foot.

5. Safety Tips:
- Stay Aware: While NYC is generally safe for tourists, it's essential to stay aware of your surroundings, especially in crowded areas.
- Secure Valuables: Keep your belongings secure to avoid pickpocketing. Use a money belt or a secure crossbody bag.
- Emergency Numbers: Familiarize yourself with emergency numbers, such as 911, and know the location of the nearest hospital or police station.

6. Language and Communication:
- English is Widely Spoken: English is the primary language in NYC, but you'll find many residents who speak other languages.
- Mobile Connectivity: Ensure your mobile phone is compatible with U.S. networks, or consider purchasing a local SIM card for data and calls.

7. Health and Safety:
   - Travel Insurance: It's wise to have travel insurance that covers medical emergencies and unexpected events.

8. Useful Resources:
   - Visitor Centers: NYC has visitor centers throughout the city, providing maps, brochures, and helpful information.
   - Official Tourism Websites: Visit NYC's official tourism websites for up-to-date information on attractions, events, and deals.
   - Mobile Apps: Download travel apps like Google Maps, NYC Subway, and ride-sharing apps for navigation and transportation.

By keeping these travel tips and resources in mind, you can make the most of your visit to New York City and create unforgettable memories in this vibrant and dynamic urban landscape.

Chapter 2. Planning Your Trip

2.1 Choosing the Right Time to Visit

Selecting the perfect time to visit New York City is crucial for a memorable experience. The city that never sleeps offers a vibrant atmosphere year-round, but each season brings its unique charm and activities. Here's a breakdown of the best times to plan your visit:

1. Spring (March to May):
   - Weather: Springtime in New York City is marked by milder temperatures and blooming flowers, making it a visually appealing season.
   - Activities: Central Park bursts with color, and outdoor attractions become more inviting. Visit in April for the beautiful cherry blossoms.
   - Events: Easter Parade, Tribeca Film Festival, and various outdoor art exhibitions.

2. Summer (June to August):
   - Weather: Expect warm to hot temperatures and occasional humidity during the summer months.
   - Activities: Summer in NYC is synonymous with outdoor fun. Enjoy free concerts in Central Park, visit Coney Island, or dine at rooftop bars.
   - Events: Shakespeare in the Park, Macy's Fourth of July Fireworks, SummerStage concerts.

3. Fall (September to November):
   - Weather: Crisp and cool weather, particularly in September and October, makes fall a delightful time to visit.
   - Activities: Central Park foliage turns into a stunning palette of autumn colors. Explore local farmers' markets and go apple-picking upstate.
   - Events: New York Film Festival, Halloween Parade, Thanksgiving Day Parade.

4. Winter (December to February):
   - Weather: Cold temperatures, occasional snowfall, and the holiday spirit dominate the winter season.
   - Activities: Ice skating at Rockefeller Center, holiday window displays, and warm up with hot chocolate at cozy cafes.
   - Events: Lighting of the Rockefeller Center Christmas Tree, New Year's Eve in Times Square.

5. Off-Peak Seasons:
   - Consider visiting during January or February for lower hotel rates and fewer crowds, but be prepared for colder weather.
   - Late summer (late August and early September) can also be a quieter time to explore the city.

Factors to Consider:
- Budget: Peak seasons tend to be more expensive. Plan your trip during off-peak times for better deals on accommodations and attractions.
- Events: Check the city's event calendar for festivals, parades, and exhibitions that align with your interests.
- Crowds: If you prefer a more relaxed visit, avoid major holidays and peak tourist seasons.
- Weather Tolerance: Assess your comfort with different weather conditions when deciding your travel dates.

Ultimately, the right time to visit New York City depends on your preferences. Whether you're captivated by spring blooms, the energy of summer, the colors of autumn, or the festive spirit of winter, NYC has something to offer year-round. Plan your trip according to your interests, and you'll undoubtedly fall in love with the Big Apple.

2.2 Creating Your Itinerary

One of the most exciting aspects of planning a trip to New York City is crafting your itinerary. The city that never sleeps offers a staggering array of attractions, activities, and experiences. Whether you're a first-time visitor or returning for another adventure, a well-structured itinerary will help you make the most of your time in the Big Apple.

Step 1: Define Your Interests

Before diving into the details of your itinerary, take a moment to identify your interests and preferences. Are you a history buff, an art enthusiast, a foodie, or an outdoor adventurer? Do you prefer a leisurely pace or a fast-paced exploration of the city? Understanding your interests will guide your itinerary planning.

Step 2: Set Realistic Goals

New York City is vast, and it's impossible to see everything in one trip. Set realistic goals for your visit based on the duration of your stay. Prioritize the top attractions and experiences you want to include while allowing some flexibility for unexpected discoveries.

Step 3: Plan by Neighborhood

New York City is divided into five boroughs, each with its own unique neighborhoods. Organize your itinerary by grouping activities in the same neighborhood to minimize travel time between sites. For example, explore Lower Manhattan's historic sites in one day, and then dedicate another day to the cultural richness of Midtown Manhattan.

Step 4: Mix Must-See with Hidden Gems

While iconic landmarks like the Statue of Liberty and Times Square are must-sees, don't forget to incorporate hidden gems and local favorites into your itinerary. Seek recommendations from locals or explore off-the-beaten-path neighborhoods to discover the city's authentic charm.

Step 5: Balance Your Days

Maintain a balance between sightseeing, relaxation, and spontaneity. Include breaks for meals, people-watching in parks, and time to simply wander the streets and soak in the city's energy. Overloading your itinerary can lead to burnout.

Step 6: Consider Timing

Check the opening hours and days of operation for attractions and restaurants. Some museums and sites may have specific days when they offer free admission or extended hours. Planning your visits accordingly can save you time and money.

Step 7: Be Weather-Prepared

New York's weather can vary significantly depending on the season, so check the forecast and pack accordingly. Have a rainy-day plan and be flexible to adjust your itinerary if the weather takes an unexpected turn.

Step 8: Embrace Local Cuisine

Include local dining experiences in your itinerary. Try classic New York foods like pizza, bagels, and street vendor hot dogs. Explore diverse neighborhoods to savor international cuisine and discover culinary gems.

Step 9: Prioritize Safety

Always prioritize safety in your itinerary. Be aware of your surroundings, avoid risky areas, and follow any local guidelines or restrictions.

Step 10: Capture the Moments

Finally, don't forget to capture your memories. Document your journey with photographs and journal entries. These mementos will help you relive your New York adventure for years to come.

Creating a well-thought-out itinerary will enhance your New York City experience and allow you to make the most of your time in this vibrant and dynamic metropolis. Enjoy your exploration of the Big Apple!

2.3 Budgeting and Expenses

New York City, often dubbed "The Big Apple," is undoubtedly an exciting destination to explore, but it can also be notorious for its high costs. However, with careful planning and smart choices, you can enjoy the city without breaking the bank. Here's a guide to budgeting and managing expenses during your visit:

1. Accommodation:
   - Consider staying in budget-friendly neighborhoods like Queens, Brooklyn, or Harlem, which often offer more affordable hotel and Airbnb options compared to Manhattan.
   - Hostels and guesthouses can be great choices for budget-conscious travelers.

2. Transportation:

- Invest in a MetroCard for the subway and buses. It provides unlimited rides for a fixed period, which can save you money compared to individual fares.
   - Explore neighborhoods on foot when possible; walking is not only budget-friendly but also the best way to soak in the city's atmosphere.

3. Dining:
   - Opt for food trucks, street vendors, and local delis for delicious and affordable meals.
   - Many restaurants offer prix-fixe menus for lunch, which can be a more budget-friendly way to enjoy a nice meal.

4. Attractions:
   - Prioritize your must-see attractions and consider purchasing a CityPASS or attraction passes for bundled discounts.
   - Take advantage of free attractions like Central Park, Times Square, and various museums that offer pay-what-you-wish or free entry on certain days.

5. Entertainment:
   - Check for discounted Broadway show tickets at TKTS booths in Times Square or consider attending off-Broadway shows for a more affordable theater experience.

- Explore free or low-cost cultural events, like public art exhibitions and outdoor concerts in parks.

6. Shopping:
  - Look for discounts at outlet malls like Woodbury Common or explore thrift shops and flea markets for unique finds at lower prices.

7. Budgeting Tools:
  - Utilize budgeting apps to keep track of your spending during your trip.
  - Set a daily spending limit and stick to it to avoid overspending.

8. Tips:
  - Always carry some cash, as some places may not accept cards.
  - Take advantage of happy hour specials at bars and restaurants for reduced drink and food prices.

9. Tipping:
  - Be aware that tipping is customary in the United States. Plan to leave a tip of around 15-20% at restaurants, bars, and for other services.

10. Emergency Fund:

- Keep a small emergency fund for unexpected expenses, like medical needs or transportation hiccups.

Remember that budgeting in New York City is about making choices that align with your priorities. By planning ahead, seeking out deals, and exploring the city with a mix of free and paid activities, you can experience the magic of NYC without straining your wallet. Enjoy your budget-friendly adventure in the city that never sleeps!

2.4 Accommodation Options

New York City offers a diverse range of accommodation options to suit every traveler's preferences and budget. Whether you're seeking luxury, comfort, or affordability, you'll find a variety of choices throughout the city. Here are some recommendations and suggestions for accommodation in New York:

1. Luxury Hotels:
   - The St. Regis New York: Experience opulence at this iconic hotel in Midtown Manhattan, known for its luxurious rooms and impeccable service.

- The Ritz-Carlton Battery Park: Enjoy stunning views of the Statue of Liberty and the harbor while indulging in world-class amenities.

2. Boutique Hotels:
   - The Greenwich Hotel: A chic and intimate hotel in Tribeca, offering uniquely designed rooms and a serene courtyard.
   - The NoMad Hotel: Located in the trendy NoMad neighborhood, this stylish boutique hotel features a stunning rooftop bar and restaurant.

3. Mid-Range Hotels:
   - Hotel Edison: Located in the heart of Times Square, this classic Art Deco hotel offers comfortable rooms and easy access to Broadway theaters.
   - The Jane Hotel: Experience a vintage New York vibe at this affordable yet charming hotel in the West Village.

4. Budget-Friendly Options:
   - HI NYC Hostel: A top choice for budget travelers, this hostel on the Upper West Side provides clean and safe accommodations with a social atmosphere.

- Pod 51 Hotel: Enjoy compact yet comfortable rooms in the heart of Manhattan, perfect for solo travelers or those looking to save on lodging.

5. Airbnb and Vacation Rentals:
   - Consider renting an apartment or a private room through Airbnb or other vacation rental platforms. This option allows you to experience New York like a local and often provides more space and amenities than traditional hotels.

6. Bed and Breakfasts:
   - The Harlem Flophouse: Stay in a charming Harlem brownstone with vintage décor and a warm, welcoming atmosphere.
   - Akwaaba Mansion: Experience historic elegance in a Brooklyn mansion turned bed and breakfast, complete with beautiful gardens.

7. Extended Stay Hotels:
   - Residence Inn by Marriott New York Downtown Manhattan/World Trade Center Area: Ideal for longer stays, these hotels offer suites with kitchenettes and additional living space.

8. Unique Stays:

- The YOTEL New York at Times Square West: Embrace the future of hospitality with its smartly designed cabins and robot luggage concierge.
- The Library Hotel: Themed after a library, each floor corresponds to a Dewey Decimal System category, making it a unique and book-lover's paradise.

Tips for Booking Accommodations in New York:
- Book well in advance, especially during peak tourist seasons.
- Consider location carefully; proximity to major attractions or public transportation can save time and money.
- Check for any additional fees, such as resort fees or city taxes, before confirming your reservation.
- Read reviews from fellow travelers to get insights into the quality and service of your chosen accommodation.

No matter your preference or budget, New York City's diverse array of accommodation options ensures you'll find the perfect place to rest your head while exploring the city that never sleeps.

2.5 Transportation in the City

New York City, renowned for its bustling streets and iconic skyline, offers a variety of transportation options to help you navigate this vibrant metropolis with ease. Whether you're a solo traveler, a family with kids, or a couple seeking a romantic getaway, understanding the city's transportation system is essential for making the most of your visit.

1. Subway: The New York City Subway is the backbone of the city's public transportation network. With an extensive network of lines and stations, it's a fast and efficient way to get around. Subway maps are readily available, and the system operates 24/7, making it convenient for late-night excursions. Be sure to purchase a MetroCard for easy access and consider downloading a subway app for real-time updates and directions.

2. Buses: NYC buses crisscross the city, serving areas not accessible by the subway. They are a great way to explore neighborhoods at a slower pace and provide a scenic view of the city. Pay your fare using a MetroCard or exact change when boarding.

3. Taxis and Rideshares: Yellow taxis are iconic in New York City and can be hailed from the street or found at designated taxi stands. Alternatively, rideshare services like Uber and Lyft are widely available. They offer a convenient option, especially

when traveling with a group or during off-peak hours.

4. Walking: NYC is a pedestrian-friendly city, and walking is often the best way to soak in the sights and sounds. Be prepared for long walks, comfortable shoes are a must. Walking is an excellent way to explore neighborhoods like SoHo, Chelsea, or the iconic Brooklyn Bridge.

5. Citi Bike: For a unique and eco-friendly experience, consider renting a Citi Bike. These bike-sharing stations are scattered throughout the city, offering a fun and healthy way to explore. The Hudson River Greenway and Central Park are perfect places for a leisurely ride.

6. Ferries: With its waterfront location, NYC offers several ferry services. The Staten Island Ferry provides stunning views of the Statue of Liberty and the Manhattan skyline. Other ferries can take you to destinations like Governors Island or the Rockaways.

7. Car Rentals: While not recommended for navigating the city's congested streets, car rentals can be useful if you plan to explore areas outside of

Manhattan. Keep in mind that parking can be expensive and challenging to find.

8. Aerial Transportation: If you're seeking a unique perspective of the city, consider a helicopter tour. These tours offer breathtaking views of the skyscrapers, bridges, and the Statue of Liberty from above.

9. Accessibility: New York City is continually improving its accessibility options for travelers with disabilities. Many subway stations are now equipped with elevators, and buses are equipped to accommodate wheelchairs. Check the official MTA website for accessibility information.

Navigating the city's transportation system may seem overwhelming at first, but with a bit of preparation and familiarity, you'll find it relatively straightforward. Regardless of your preferred mode of transportation, New York City's diverse neighborhoods and attractions are waiting to be explored.

Chapter 3. New York City Overview

3.1 Geographical Layout

New York City, often referred to as "The Big Apple," is not only one of the most iconic cities in the world but also one of the most diverse in terms of its geographical layout. Understanding the city's layout is essential for any traveler looking to explore its various neighborhoods and attractions.

1. Boroughs: New York City is composed of five boroughs, each with its own distinct character. These boroughs are:
   - Manhattan: Known as the city's economic and cultural center, Manhattan is home to iconic landmarks like Times Square, Central Park, and the Financial District.
   - Brooklyn: Famous for its trendy neighborhoods, Brooklyn offers a vibrant arts scene, historic brownstones, and stunning views of the Manhattan skyline.
   - Queens: The most ethnically diverse borough, Queens boasts excellent food, cultural festivals, and attractions such as Flushing Meadows-Corona Park.
   - The Bronx: Home to the Bronx Zoo and Yankee Stadium, this borough is rich in history and culture, with beautiful parks and museums.

- Staten Island: Known for its natural beauty, Staten Island offers hiking trails, the Staten Island Ferry, and the stunning Snug Harbor Cultural Center.

2. Manhattan's Street Grid: Manhattan's layout follows a grid system with streets running east to west and avenues running north to south. Streets are numbered, making navigation relatively straightforward.

3. Waterways: New York City is surrounded by water, with the Hudson River on the west and the East River on the east. The city's many bridges and tunnels connect the boroughs, creating picturesque views and essential transportation links.

4. Central Park: At the heart of Manhattan, Central Park is a massive green oasis that provides a stark contrast to the city's skyscrapers. It's a popular spot for outdoor activities, picnics, and leisurely strolls.

5. Neighborhoods: New York City is a city of neighborhoods, each with its own unique charm. From the artsy vibe of Greenwich Village to the historic architecture of Harlem, there's something for everyone.

6. Islands: Beyond the five main boroughs, New York City includes smaller islands like Roosevelt Island and Governors Island, each offering its own attractions and experiences.

7. Elevation: While much of the city is relatively flat, there are areas with varying elevations. For instance, the Upper Manhattan area is hilly, providing elevated viewpoints of the city.

Understanding the geographical layout of New York City is crucial for planning your visit. It allows you to navigate the city efficiently, explore its diverse neighborhoods, and appreciate the unique character of each borough. Whether you're exploring the bustling streets of Manhattan or the cultural enclaves of Queens, New York City's geographical diversity ensures there's always something new to discover around every corner.

3.2 Neighborhoods and Boroughs

New York City is a vast metropolis made up of five distinct boroughs, each with its own unique charm and personality. Understanding the neighborhoods and boroughs is essential for making the most of your visit to the Big Apple.

1. Manhattan

- Midtown: The heart of Manhattan, home to iconic landmarks like Times Square, Broadway theaters, and Rockefeller Center.
- Lower Manhattan: Discover the historic Financial District, Wall Street, and the poignant 9/11 Memorial.
- Upper East Side and Upper West Side: Explore cultural institutions like the Metropolitan Museum of Art and Central Park.
- Greenwich Village and SoHo: Experience artistic vibes, boutique shopping, and delicious dining.
- Harlem: Immerse yourself in Harlem's rich history, music scene, and soul food.

2. Brooklyn
- Williamsburg: A hipster haven with trendy cafes, street art, and scenic views of Manhattan.
- DUMBO: Admire the Manhattan Bridge, visit art galleries, and stroll along the picturesque Brooklyn Bridge Park.
- Park Slope: Family-friendly neighborhood known for its leafy streets, Prospect Park, and local boutiques.
- Coney Island: Enjoy classic amusements, a historic boardwalk, and a day at the beach.

3. Queens

- Flushing: A diverse neighborhood with excellent Asian cuisine, cultural festivals, and Flushing Meadows-Corona Park.
  - Long Island City: Home to art galleries, waterfront parks, and stunning views of the Manhattan skyline.
  - Astoria: Experience Greek culture, great food, and the Museum of the Moving Image.
  - Jackson Heights: Explore global cuisine, diverse communities, and beautiful gardens.

4. The Bronx
  - The Bronx Zoo: Visit one of the largest metropolitan zoos in the world.
  - Arthur Avenue: Savor Italian cuisine and explore the "real Little Italy" of New York.
  - Yankee Stadium: Catch a baseball game at the iconic home of the New York Yankees.

5. Staten Island
  - St. George: Take the Staten Island Ferry for fantastic views of the Statue of Liberty and Manhattan.
  - Snug Harbor Cultural Center: Enjoy botanical gardens, museums, and historic architecture.
  - Conference House Park: Explore the serene southern tip of Staten Island.

Navigating New York City's neighborhoods and boroughs allows you to experience the city's incredible diversity. Each area offers its own set of attractions, from world-renowned landmarks to hidden gems waiting to be discovered. Whether you're exploring the bustling streets of Manhattan or the artistic enclaves of Brooklyn, you're sure to find something that captures your heart in the City that Never Sleeps.

3.3 Weather and Climate

New York City experiences a diverse range of weather conditions throughout the year, offering travelers a unique experience in each season. Understanding the climate and weather patterns can help you plan your trip effectively.

Seasons:
1. Spring (March to May): Spring in New York is a delightful time to visit as the city comes alive with blossoming flowers and milder temperatures. Average highs range from 50°F (10°C) in March to 70°F (21°C) in May. Be prepared for occasional rain showers.

2. Summer (June to August): New York summers are known for their warmth and humidity. Average highs can reach 80-85°F (27-30°C), occasionally

soaring higher. This is a popular time for tourists, so expect larger crowds at attractions.

3. Fall (September to November): Fall is a beautiful time to explore New York City. The weather is pleasant, with temperatures ranging from 60-70°F (15-21°C) in September to 40-50°F (4-10°C) in November. The city's foliage turns into a stunning array of autumn colors.

4. Winter (December to February): New York winters can be chilly and snowfall is common, especially in January and February. Average highs are around 40°F (4°C), but it can drop below freezing. It's a great time for holiday festivities and ice skating in iconic locations like Rockefeller Center.

Precipitation:
Rainfall is relatively evenly distributed throughout the year, with slightly more precipitation during the summer months. Snowfall, on the other hand, is typical in the winter, making the city a winter wonderland.

Extreme Weather Events:
New York City can experience occasional extreme weather events, including heavy snowstorms,

hurricanes, and heatwaves. While these events are relatively rare, it's essential to stay informed about local weather forecasts during your visit, especially in the winter and hurricane season.

Packing Tips:
- Spring and Fall: Layered clothing is key to adapt to changing temperatures. An umbrella and a light jacket are recommended.
- Summer: Lightweight clothing, sunscreen, and sunglasses are essential for the heat. Don't forget to stay hydrated.
- Winter: Warm clothing, including a heavy coat, gloves, and a hat, is a must. Sturdy, waterproof boots are advisable if you plan to navigate snowy streets.

In conclusion, New York City's weather and climate offer a unique experience in each season. Whether you prefer the vibrant blooms of spring, the warmth of summer, the colors of autumn, or the magic of a snowy winter, the city has something to offer year-round. Be sure to check the weather forecast before your trip and pack accordingly to make the most of your visit to the Big Apple.

Chapter 4. Solo Travelers

4.1 Safety Tips

New York City is a vibrant and exciting destination, but like any major urban center, it's important for solo travelers to be mindful of safety. Here are some essential safety tips to keep in mind when exploring the Big Apple alone:

1. Stay Aware of Your Surroundings: One of the most important safety practices is to always stay alert. Keep an eye on your belongings, know where you are at all times, and be aware of the people around you.

2. Choose Accommodations Wisely: When booking a place to stay, research the neighborhood and read reviews. Opt for well-reviewed hotels or hostels in safe areas. It's often a good idea to stay in neighborhoods like Midtown Manhattan or parts of Brooklyn known for their safety.

3. Use Reputable Transportation: Stick to official taxis, ride-sharing services, or public transportation. Avoid accepting rides from strangers, especially if they approach you on the street.

4. Secure Your Valuables: Keep your passport, important documents, and most of your cash locked in a hotel safe. When you're out and about, carry only what you need and use a money belt or hidden pouch to store valuables.

5. Stay on Well-Lit Streets: At night, stick to well-lit and busy streets. Avoid taking shortcuts through dark alleys or deserted areas, even if it means a slightly longer walk.

6. Avoid Flashy Displays of Wealth: NYC is known for its fashion, but consider toning down flashy jewelry or designer labels to avoid drawing unnecessary attention to yourself.

7. Trust Your Instincts: If something doesn't feel right or if someone makes you uncomfortable, don't hesitate to remove yourself from the situation. Trust your gut.

8. Share Your Itinerary: Let a friend or family member know your daily plans and whereabouts. Share your itinerary and check-in with them regularly.

9. Use Technology Wisely: Keep your phone charged and use it for navigation and emergency calls. Download offline maps in case you lose signal.

10. Be Cautious with Alcohol: If you choose to consume alcohol, do so responsibly. Be mindful of your limits and always keep an eye on your drink to prevent tampering.

11. Learn Basic Phrases: Familiarize yourself with basic phrases in English, as well as common local slang, to enhance your communication and understanding of your surroundings.

12. Join Group Activities: Consider joining group tours or activities during your trip. Not only do they offer great opportunities to meet fellow travelers, but they also provide an added layer of safety.

13. Know Emergency Numbers: Be aware of the local emergency numbers, which are 911 in the United States. Have this number saved in your phone for quick access.

By following these safety tips, solo travelers can enjoy their New York City adventure with confidence, knowing they're taking steps to stay safe and make the most of their visit to this iconic destination.

4.2 Solo-Friendly Activities

New York City, with its vibrant energy and endless possibilities, is a fantastic destination for solo travelers. Exploring the city on your own can be a deeply enriching experience. Here are some solo-friendly activities to make the most of your solo adventure in the Big Apple:

1. Walking Tours: Join a guided walking tour to discover the city's neighborhoods, history, and hidden gems. From the historic streets of Lower Manhattan to the artistic haven of Chelsea, there are tours for every interest.

2. Central Park Strolls: Escape the hustle and bustle by taking leisurely walks through Central Park. You can visit iconic spots like Bethesda Terrace, Strawberry Fields, or simply find a quiet bench and people-watch.

3. Museum Exploration: New York boasts world-class museums, and solo travelers can immerse themselves in art and culture. The Met, MoMA, and the Whitney Museum are perfect places to spend hours appreciating art and history.

4. Solo Dining Adventures: New York is a culinary paradise. Don't hesitate to dine alone – it's a common practice. Try diverse cuisines in local eateries or savor street food while chatting with food truck vendors.

5. Broadway Solo: Treat yourself to a solo night out on Broadway. Purchase a single ticket to a show, and immerse yourself in the magic of live theater.

6. Explore the Boroughs: Venture beyond Manhattan to discover the unique charm of Brooklyn, Queens, the Bronx, and Staten Island. Each borough has its own distinct personality and attractions.

7. Hudson River Park: Enjoy a peaceful walk along the Hudson River Park Greenway. This scenic path offers breathtaking views of the river and the city skyline.

8. Visit Bookstores: Book lovers can explore independent bookstores like The Strand or McNally Jackson, where you can get lost in the shelves for hours.

9. Visit the 9/11 Memorial: Pay your respects at the 9/11 Memorial and Museum. It's a solemn and reflective experience that solo travelers often find moving.

10. Take a Ferry Ride: Hop on a ferry to see the Statue of Liberty or Ellis Island. The boat ride provides a unique perspective of these iconic landmarks.

11. Attend Meetup Events: Check out local meetup groups and events for solo travelers. It's a great way to meet like-minded individuals and make new friends.

12. Photography Expeditions: Capture the essence of New York through your lens. Explore the city with your camera and take stunning photographs of iconic landmarks.

Remember, solo travel in New York City is all about embracing your independence and exploring the city at your own pace. Don't hesitate to strike up conversations with locals or fellow travelers along the way – you might just make some unforgettable connections during your solo adventure in the city that never sleeps.

4.3 Dining Alone

One of the many charms of New York City is its vibrant dining scene, and as a solo traveler, you have the unique opportunity to explore it at your own pace. Dining alone in the Big Apple can be an enriching experience, offering you a chance to savor the diverse culinary delights while immersing yourself in the city's eclectic atmosphere.

1. Embrace the Bar
   - Many restaurants in New York City have welcoming bar areas where solo diners can feel comfortable. Sitting at the bar offers a chance to engage in conversation with friendly bartenders or fellow patrons.
   - Try some of the city's signature cocktails or indulge in a glass of wine while enjoying your meal.

2. Choose a Variety of Cuisine
   - New York City is a melting pot of cultures and cuisines, so take advantage of this diversity. From pizza slices to international fine dining, there's something for every palate.
   - Don't miss the chance to sample classic New York dishes like a bagel with lox or a slice of iconic New York-style pizza.

3. Brunch and Breakfast Spots

- NYC is renowned for its brunch culture. Enjoy a leisurely brunch at one of the city's trendy cafes or brunch spots. It's an excellent opportunity to people-watch and savor a delicious meal.
   - Try classic brunch options like eggs benedict, avocado toast, or a hearty New York-style breakfast sandwich.

4. Food Markets and Street Food
   - Explore food markets like Chelsea Market or Smorgasburg in Williamsburg, Brooklyn. These markets offer a wide range of culinary options from local and international vendors.
   - NYC's street food scene is legendary. Grab a hot dog from a food cart, indulge in a pretzel, or savor some of the city's best food truck offerings.

5. Reservation or Walk-In?
   - While dining solo often means you can be more flexible with your plans, it's still a good idea to make reservations for popular restaurants, especially during peak dining hours.
   - For spontaneous meals, New York City has numerous walk-in-friendly eateries where you can enjoy a meal without prior planning.

6. Dining with a View

- Consider dining at a restaurant with a view. There are several rooftop bars and restaurants that offer stunning vistas of the city's skyline, making your solo dining experience even more memorable.

7. Engage with Locals
   - Don't hesitate to strike up a conversation with locals or fellow solo travelers. New Yorkers are known for their friendliness and may offer you valuable recommendations or insights into the city.

8. Reading Material or People Watching
   - Bring a book or simply enjoy people-watching as you dine. New York City's diverse and bustling streets provide endless entertainment.

9. Safety Tips
   - While New York City is generally safe for solo travelers, it's always a good practice to be cautious with your belongings and surroundings, especially in crowded areas.

Dining alone in New York City is not just a culinary experience; it's a chance to soak in the city's energy and embrace the freedom of solo travel. Whether you're enjoying a slice of pizza on a park bench or indulging in a multi-course meal at a Michelin-starred restaurant, dining alone in the city that never sleeps can be an unforgettable adventure.

4.4 Meeting Locals and Fellow Travelers

One of the most enriching aspects of solo travel is the opportunity to connect with locals and fellow adventurers. In the bustling metropolis of New York City, making meaningful connections with people from diverse backgrounds is an experience that can add a unique dimension to your journey. Here are some tips and ideas for meeting locals and fellow travelers in the Big Apple:

1. Join Guided Tours: New York City offers an abundance of guided tours, ranging from historical walking tours to food tasting excursions. These tours not only introduce you to the city's attractions but also provide a chance to interact with both knowledgeable guides and fellow tourists. It's a great way to strike up conversations and share travel experiences.

2. Stay in Social Accommodations: Opt for accommodations that promote social interactions, such as hostels, boutique hotels with communal spaces, or Airbnb experiences where you can stay with a local host. These settings often encourage mingling with other travelers and residents.

3. Attend Local Events: Check out local event listings for concerts, art exhibitions, and community gatherings. Places like Central Park, Bryant Park, and various museums often host free events and performances. Engaging in these activities can lead to spontaneous conversations with locals who share your interests.

4. Visit Neighborhood Cafes and Bars: New York City is renowned for its diverse culinary scene. Frequenting neighborhood cafes and bars can provide a laid-back environment to chat with locals. Strike up conversations with bartenders or fellow patrons; you might discover hidden gems or receive insider tips on the city.

5. Join Social Media Groups: Utilize social media platforms or online forums to connect with fellow travelers visiting New York City during the same timeframe. Many cities have specific Facebook groups or Reddit communities dedicated to travelers looking for companions, advice, or meet-ups.

6. Volunteer: Consider spending some time volunteering during your visit. New York City has numerous volunteer opportunities, from food banks

to community gardens. Not only will you contribute to a good cause, but you'll also have the chance to interact with locals who share your commitment to helping others.

7. Language Exchange Meetups: If you're interested in learning a new language or practicing one you already know, language exchange meetups are a fantastic way to meet people. New Yorkers hail from all corners of the globe, so you're likely to find language exchange partners.

8. Public Transportation Conversations: Strike up conversations with fellow commuters on the subway or while waiting for buses. New Yorkers are known for their fast-paced lives, but many are open to a friendly chat if you're respectful of their space and time.

Remember, New Yorkers are diverse, open-minded, and often welcoming to travelers. Be friendly, approachable, and respectful of local customs, and you'll likely find yourself engaged in meaningful conversations and making memorable connections that enhance your solo adventure in the city that never sleeps.

Chapter 5. Traveling with Kids

5.1 Family-Friendly Attractions

New York City may be famous for its bustling streets and towering skyscrapers, but it's also a fantastic destination for families with kids. The city offers a diverse range of family-friendly attractions that cater to various ages and interests. Here, we explore some of the top places to visit with your family in the Big Apple:

1. Central Park
   - Central Park is a vast green oasis in the heart of Manhattan, providing a serene escape from the urban jungle. Families can enjoy picnics, paddle boating on the lake, and visiting iconic spots like the Central Park Zoo, which houses a variety of animals.

2. American Museum of Natural History
   - This world-renowned museum is a treasure trove of scientific wonders. Kids can marvel at the massive dinosaur fossils, explore the Butterfly Conservatory, and learn about the universe at the Hayden Planetarium.

3. The Intrepid Sea, Air & Space Museum

- Located aboard the USS Intrepid aircraft carrier, this museum offers a unique opportunity for kids to explore historic aircraft, submarines, and even a Concorde jet. The interactive exhibits provide hands-on learning experiences for all ages.

4. Children's Museum of Manhattan
 - Designed especially for children, this museum encourages interactive learning through art, science, and play. It features numerous exhibits, including Dora and Diego, PlayWorks, and the Tisch Building for art exploration.

5. Bronx Zoo
 - The Bronx Zoo is one of the largest metropolitan zoos in the world. Families can spend hours observing animals from around the globe, including tigers, giraffes, and penguins. Don't miss the Bug Carousel and the Children's Zoo.

6. Empire State Building
 - A visit to the Empire State Building is an iconic New York experience. While kids may not fully grasp the historical significance, they'll certainly appreciate the breathtaking views from the observation deck.

7. Coney Island

- This historic amusement park by the beach is a summer favorite. It offers thrilling rides, carnival games, and the world-famous Cyclone roller coaster. The boardwalk and beach provide additional opportunities for family fun.

8. Staten Island Ferry
   - Take a free ride on the Staten Island Ferry for stunning views of the Statue of Liberty and the Manhattan skyline. It's a short and enjoyable trip for kids, and you can return on the same ferry.

9. New York Aquarium
   - Located in Coney Island, the New York Aquarium showcases marine life from around the world. Kids can watch playful sea otters, colorful fish, and even visit the interactive Aquatheater for a live animal show.

10. Children's Shows
    - NYC is famous for its Broadway productions, but it also offers family-friendly shows like "The Lion King" and "Aladdin." These captivating performances will enchant kids and adults alike.

New York City's family-friendly attractions ensure that everyone, from the youngest to the oldest members of the family, can enjoy an unforgettable adventure in the city that never sleeps. Whether you're exploring nature in Central Park, discovering history at museums, or seeking thrills at amusement parks, NYC has something special for every family.

5.2 Kid-Friendly Dining

New York City is not only a haven for foodies but also a fantastic place to dine with the whole family, including the little ones. Whether you have picky eaters or adventurous young palates, the city offers a wide range of kid-friendly dining options that cater to children of all ages. Here are some tips and recommendations for enjoying family meals in the Big Apple:

1. Kid's Menus: Many restaurants in New York City have dedicated kid's menus. These menus typically feature familiar favorites like chicken tenders, mac 'n' cheese, and mini burgers, ensuring that even the fussiest eaters find something they love.

2. Family-Friendly Neighborhoods: Consider dining in family-friendly neighborhoods like the Upper West Side, Park Slope in Brooklyn, or the Upper East Side. These areas often have a wealth of family-oriented restaurants, and you'll find other families dining there too.

3. Food Trucks: Don't overlook the city's food trucks and street vendors. They offer quick and delicious options like hot dogs, pretzels, and ice cream, perfect for satisfying hungry kids on the go.

4. Diners: New York City's classic diners are not only iconic but also kid-friendly. They serve up breakfast classics like pancakes, waffles, and omelets at all hours, making them ideal for families with early risers.

5. Interactive Dining: Consider restaurants with interactive dining experiences like Benihana or The Rainforest Cafe. These places often have entertaining chefs or themed decor that can capture children's imaginations.

6. Pizza Places: New York-style pizza is a hit with kids and adults alike. Head to one of the many pizzerias around the city and enjoy a slice of this iconic dish.

7. Ice Cream Shops: Treat your kids to some of the best ice cream in the world at renowned places like Serendipity 3, where they can savor massive sundaes and whimsical frozen desserts.

8. Cafeterias: For a casual and budget-friendly option, explore cafeteria-style dining establishments like Shake Shack or Eataly's La Piazza. These spots offer a variety of choices and fast service.

9. Themed Restaurants: New York City boasts themed restaurants like Ellen's Stardust Diner, where aspiring Broadway stars serve your meals while singing show tunes, creating a memorable experience for the whole family.

10. Outdoor Dining: During pleasant weather, take advantage of outdoor dining options in parks or restaurants with outdoor seating. It's a great way for kids to enjoy their meal while soaking in the city's atmosphere.

Safety Note: Always ensure the restaurant you choose follows health and safety guidelines, especially if you have young children. Many restaurants have outdoor seating and takeout options to accommodate families more comfortably.

In New York City, you'll find that dining with kids can be both enjoyable and stress-free. With a plethora of family-friendly dining establishments and an array of cuisines to choose from, your little ones will have the opportunity to savor the city's culinary delights while making unforgettable memories.

5.3 Practical Tips for Parents

Traveling to New York City with children can be an exciting adventure, but it also comes with its own set of challenges. To ensure a smooth and enjoyable trip for both you and your kids, here are some practical tips to consider:

1. Choose Kid-Friendly Accommodations
   - Look for family-friendly hotels or vacation rentals that offer amenities like cribs, high chairs, and kid-friendly menus.
   - Check if the hotel has a pool or outdoor space where your kids can unwind.

2. Plan Kid-Centric Activities
   - Research and prioritize attractions suitable for children, such as Central Park, the Bronx Zoo, and the American Museum of Natural History.
   - Consider interactive museums like the Children's Museum of Manhattan or the Intrepid Sea, Air & Space Museum.

3. Prepare for Walking

- New York City involves a lot of walking. Ensure your kids have comfortable walking shoes, and use a stroller for younger ones.
  - Plan shorter walking routes and frequent breaks for snacks and rest.

4. Timing Matters
  - Visit popular attractions early in the day to avoid crowds and long lines.
  - Keep in mind the weather, especially during extreme heat or cold, and plan indoor activities as needed.

5. Bring Essentials
  - Pack a backpack with essentials like diapers, wipes, a change of clothes, snacks, and water bottles.
  - Consider a baby carrier or sling for younger children, as navigating crowded areas with strollers can be challenging.

6. Dining with Kids
  - Look for restaurants with kid-friendly menus and high chairs.
  - Inform servers of any dietary restrictions or allergies your child may have.

7. Public Transportation

- Familiarize yourself with the subway system and buses. Most subway stations have elevators or escalators for stroller access.
  - Consider purchasing a MetroCard for convenient travel.

8. Be Safety Conscious
  - Teach your children about pedestrian safety and holding hands in busy areas.
  - Have a plan in case you get separated, such as a designated meeting spot.

9. Entertainment on the Go
  - Bring entertainment for kids during downtime, like coloring books, puzzles, or electronic devices with headphones.
  - NYC has many parks and playgrounds where kids can burn off energy.

10. Stay Flexible
  - Be prepared for changes in plans. Sometimes the unexpected can lead to delightful discoveries.
  - Prioritize your child's comfort and enjoyment over sticking rigidly to an itinerary.

11. Seek Child-Friendly Services
  - Utilize family restrooms when available for diaper changes.

- Many attractions offer stroller parking, making it easier to explore without the stroller.

12. Capture Memories
- Document your family's adventures with photos and videos to create lasting memories.
- Encourage your kids to keep a travel journal or draw pictures of their experiences.

Traveling with kids in New York City can be incredibly rewarding. By planning ahead, staying adaptable, and embracing the city's kid-friendly offerings, you'll create memorable experiences that your children will cherish for a lifetime.

Chapter 6. Couples' Getaway

6.1 Romantic Spots

New York City, often referred to as the "City of Love," offers a plethora of romantic settings for couples seeking a memorable getaway. Whether you're strolling hand in hand through iconic parks or sharing a candlelit dinner with a breathtaking skyline view, the city provides an enchanting backdrop for lovebirds. Here are some of the most romantic spots to explore:

1. Central Park
    * Central Park is a haven for romance. Take a leisurely rowboat ride on the Central Park Lake or enjoy a peaceful picnic in the Sheep Meadow. The Bow Bridge is a classic spot for proposals and romantic moments.

2. Brooklyn Bridge
    * Walk hand in hand across the iconic Brooklyn Bridge at sunset or under the twinkling lights at night. The view of the Manhattan skyline from the bridge is nothing short of magical.

3. Top of the Rock
    * Head to the Top of the Rock Observation Deck at Rockefeller Center for a panoramic view of the

city. Sunset or nighttime visits are particularly romantic, offering a dazzling cityscape.

4. The High Line
   * The High Line is an elevated park built on an old railway track, offering a unique perspective of the city. Wander through beautifully landscaped gardens and enjoy the art installations along the way.

5. Empire State Building
   * The Empire State Building's Observation Deck is another top choice for couples. The city lights create a mesmerizing atmosphere, making it a popular spot for proposals.

6. The Metropolitan Museum of Art
   * Explore the art world together at The Met. The museum's grand halls, exquisite sculptures, and impressive collections provide a cultural and romantic experience.

7. Romantic Dining
   * New York City boasts a vast array of romantic restaurants. Dine with your loved one at candlelit tables with spectacular views. Some favorites include One if by Land, Two if by Sea, and River Café.

8. The Cloisters
   * Located in Fort Tryon Park, The Cloisters is a museum dedicated to medieval art. The tranquil gardens and historic architecture create a serene and romantic atmosphere.

9. Grand Central Terminal
   * Grand Central Terminal's celestial ceiling and grand architecture set the stage for a romantic rendezvous. Whisper sweet nothings at the Whispering Gallery for a unique experience.

10. Boat Rides
    * Take a romantic boat ride in the city. Options include the Staten Island Ferry, evening cruises, or even a private sail on the Hudson River.

Whether you're celebrating a special occasion, planning a proposal, or simply cherishing your time together, New York City's romantic spots provide the perfect setting for love to flourish. Don't forget to capture these moments in the city that never sleeps, as they are sure to be treasured memories for years to come.

6.2 Dining and Date Night Ideas

New York City is not only renowned for its iconic landmarks and vibrant cultural scene but also for its world-class dining experiences, making it the perfect destination for a romantic date night. Whether you're seeking a cozy spot for an intimate dinner or a unique culinary adventure, the city that never sleeps has it all. Here are some dining and date night ideas to elevate your NYC experience:

1. Fine Dining with a View:
   - One Dine: Located in One World Trade Center, enjoy a sophisticated meal with breathtaking panoramic views of the city.
   - River Café: Nestled under the Brooklyn Bridge, this Michelin-starred restaurant offers a romantic setting overlooking the Manhattan skyline.

2. Candlelit Charm:
   - Gramercy Tavern: Known for its warm ambiance and seasonal American cuisine, it's perfect for a classic, candlelit dinner.
   - Bar Boulud: Experience French culinary delights in an intimate atmosphere on the Upper West Side.

3. Hidden Gems:

- Angel's Share: A hidden speakeasy in the East Village with exceptional cocktails and an intimate setting.
  - Freemans: Tucked away in a cozy alley on the Lower East Side, this rustic American restaurant offers an enchanting escape from the city hustle.

4. Culinary Adventures:
  - Chelsea Market: Explore this food hall for diverse dining options and discover artisanal treats together.
  - Smorgasburg: If your date falls on a weekend, visit this open-air food market in Williamsburg or Prospect Park for a taste of NYC's street food scene.

5. Romantic Rooftop Bars:
  - 230 Fifth Rooftop Bar: Sip cocktails amidst heated igloos with stunning views of the Empire State Building.
  - The Press Lounge: Enjoy a sophisticated evening with a view of the Hudson River and Manhattan skyline.

6. Cooking Classes:
  - The Brooklyn Kitchen: Learn to cook a meal together and bond over a shared culinary experience.

- Miette Culinary Studio: Explore a variety of cooking classes, from sushi-making to pasta workshops.

7. Dinner Cruises:
  - Bateaux New York: Sail along the Hudson River while savoring a gourmet dinner and live music.
  - Spirit of New York: Dance the night away on a dinner cruise with dazzling city views.

8. Theater and Dining:
  - Restaurant Row: Enjoy pre-show dining in the Theater District, where you'll find a plethora of restaurants to choose from before catching a Broadway performance.

9. Dessert Delights:
  - Milk Bar: Satisfy your sweet tooth with inventive desserts like the famous Compost Cookie.
  - Serendipity 3: Share the famous Frozen Hot Chocolate at this whimsical dessert spot.

10. Artful Dining:
  - The Modern: Combine art and cuisine with a visit to the Museum of Modern Art's fine dining restaurant.
  - Rainbow Room: Dine and dance in this iconic venue at the Rockefeller Center.

No matter your culinary preference or budget, New York City offers a plethora of dining and date night options that cater to every romantic occasion. From cozy corners to world-class cuisine, the city's diverse food scene will undoubtedly enhance your love story in the heart of the Big Apple.

6.3 Planning a Memorable Proposal

New York City, with its iconic skyline, romantic ambiance, and countless picturesque settings, is a dream location for those looking to pop the question and create a cherished memory. Here's how to plan a memorable proposal in the city that never sleeps:

1. Choose the Perfect Location: New York offers a myriad of stunning proposal spots. Consider classic locations like Central Park, with its scenic bridges and lakeside views, or the Brooklyn Bridge, offering a backdrop of the Manhattan skyline. Other options include the Top of the Rock at Rockefeller Center, the High Line, or even a horse-drawn carriage ride through Central Park.

2. Time it Right: Timing is crucial for a perfect proposal. The soft glow of sunset or the twinkling lights of the city at night can add a magical touch to

your moment. Plan your proposal for a time that suits your chosen location and the atmosphere you desire.

3. Capture the Moment: Arrange for a discreet photographer or videographer to capture the proposal. Alternatively, ask a friendly passerby to snap a photo or record a video. Having these memories preserved will make your proposal even more special.

4. Add Personal Touches: Incorporate personal elements into your proposal. This could include sentimental items, a heartfelt letter, or your favorite song playing in the background. Tailoring the moment to reflect your relationship will make it truly unforgettable.

5. Plan the Aftermath: After the proposal, consider where you'll celebrate. Many couples choose to dine at a romantic restaurant or enjoy a champagne toast. Make a reservation in advance to ensure you have a table waiting for you.

6. Engagement Photoshoot: If you've hired a photographer, extend the shoot to capture engagement photos at various iconic NYC locations.

This way, you'll have a beautiful collection of images to remember the day.

7. Share the News: Notify friends and family before posting your engagement on social media. This personal touch ensures your loved ones hear the news directly from you.

8. Consider Allergies and Preferences: If you plan to propose with food or flowers, be aware of any allergies or dietary preferences your partner may have to ensure the moment goes off without a hitch.

9. Keep it a Surprise: The element of surprise can make a proposal even more memorable. Plan discreetly, and if necessary, enlist the help of a friend or family member to keep the secret.

10. Stay Calm: Remember that proposals are emotional, and your partner will appreciate sincerity over perfection. Stay calm and focus on the love you share.

A New York City proposal is an unforgettable experience that you and your partner will treasure forever. With careful planning and a touch of romance, you can create a moment that sets the stage for a lifetime of love and happiness in this remarkable city.

Chapter 7. Must-See Attractions

7.1 Iconic Landmarks

New York City is a treasure trove of iconic landmarks that have become symbols of the city itself. From towering skyscrapers to historic monuments, these landmarks are a testament to the city's rich history and vibrant culture. Here are some of the most iconic landmarks you simply can't miss when visiting the Big Apple:

1. Statue of Liberty: A symbol of freedom and democracy, Lady Liberty stands proudly in New York Harbor. Visitors can take a ferry to Liberty Island to get up close and explore the statue and its pedestal, and enjoy breathtaking views of the city skyline.

2. Empire State Building: This world-famous skyscraper offers panoramic views of the city from its observation deck. It's especially stunning at sunset or nighttime when the city lights come alive.

3. Times Square: Known as "The Crossroads of the World," Times Square is a bustling hub of entertainment, shopping, and bright electronic billboards. It's the place to be on New Year's Eve

when the famous ball drop welcomes in the new year.

4. Brooklyn Bridge: An architectural marvel, this historic suspension bridge connects Manhattan and Brooklyn. A stroll or bike ride across it offers breathtaking views of the skyline and the East River.

5. Central Park: This massive urban park is an oasis in the heart of Manhattan. It's home to lush greenery, scenic lakes, art installations, and numerous attractions, including the Central Park Zoo.

6. One World Trade Center: Also known as the Freedom Tower, this modern skyscraper was built to replace the Twin Towers destroyed on 9/11. Its observatory provides a moving experience and incredible views of the city.

7. Rockefeller Center: Famous for its Christmas tree lighting ceremony, this iconic complex includes Radio City Music Hall, the Top of the Rock Observatory, and the stunning Prometheus statue.

8. The Metropolitan Museum of Art: The Met is one of the largest and most prestigious art museums in

the world. It boasts an extensive collection of art spanning centuries and cultures.

9. The Museum of Modern Art (MoMA): For lovers of contemporary and modern art, MoMA is a must-visit. It houses works by renowned artists like Picasso, Van Gogh, and Warhol.

10. Charging Bull: This iconic bronze sculpture in the Financial District represents the strength and optimism of Wall Street. It's a popular spot for photos and a symbol of financial prosperity.

11. St. Patrick's Cathedral: A masterpiece of Gothic architecture, this cathedral on Fifth Avenue is a serene contrast to the bustling city. Visitors can explore its stunning interior and attend mass.

12. The Flatiron Building: This triangular-shaped skyscraper is a true architectural gem and a symbol of New York's innovative spirit.

These iconic landmarks not only define the city's skyline but also its cultural identity. Exploring these sites provides an unforgettable glimpse into the history, art, and vibrancy of New York City.

7.2 *Museums and Art Galleries*

New York City is a cultural powerhouse with an unrivaled wealth of museums and art galleries that cater to every taste and interest. From iconic institutions housing priceless masterpieces to contemporary art spaces pushing the boundaries of creativity, the city's cultural scene is nothing short of impressive. Here are some of the must-visit museums and galleries that should be on every traveler's itinerary:

1. The Metropolitan Museum of Art (The Met):
   - Known simply as "The Met," this museum is one of the world's largest and most prestigious art museums. It boasts a vast collection that spans over 5,000 years of art, featuring everything from ancient Egyptian artifacts to European masterpieces. Don't miss the Temple of Dendur or the incredible array of Impressionist paintings.

2. The Museum of Modern Art (MoMA):
   - MoMA is a haven for modern and contemporary art enthusiasts. It houses an exceptional collection of works by artists like Picasso, Van Gogh, and Warhol. The museum's rotating exhibitions ensure there's always something new to discover.

3. The Solomon R. Guggenheim Museum:

- Designed by Frank Lloyd Wright, the Guggenheim is as much an architectural marvel as it is a museum. Inside, you'll find an impressive collection of modern and contemporary art, including pieces by Kandinsky and Pollock.

4. The Whitney Museum of American Art:
   - Focusing on 20th and 21st-century American art, the Whitney is known for showcasing the works of emerging artists alongside established ones. Its location in the trendy Meatpacking District adds to its appeal.

5. The Museum of Natural History:
   - Perfect for families, this museum is home to fascinating exhibits on everything from dinosaurs to space exploration. The iconic dioramas and the giant blue whale in the Hall of Ocean Life are highlights.

6. The Frick Collection:
   - Housed in a former Gilded Age mansion, the Frick Collection offers an intimate art experience. It features a remarkable collection of European paintings, sculptures, and decorative arts.

7. The Brooklyn Museum:

- Located in the heart of Brooklyn's cultural district, this museum boasts an extensive collection of art and artifacts, including impressive Egyptian holdings and contemporary art exhibitions.

8. The New Museum:
   - For cutting-edge contemporary art, head to the New Museum in the Lower East Side. It showcases works by emerging and established artists, often pushing boundaries and challenging norms.

9. The MoMA PS1:
   - A satellite of MoMA, PS1 is dedicated to contemporary and experimental art. Its gritty yet innovative atmosphere is a must-visit for those interested in avant-garde works.

10. The Rubin Museum of Art:
   - Explore the art, culture, and spirituality of the Himalayas at the Rubin Museum. It's a serene and enlightening experience right in the heart of Manhattan.

These are just a few of the many museums and galleries that grace the cultural landscape of New York City. Whether you're a seasoned art aficionado or simply curious about the world of creativity, New York's museums and galleries offer a diverse and enriching experience for all visitors. Be sure to check opening hours and any reservation requirements, as they may vary.

7.3 Parks and Outdoor Activities

New York City, often associated with its iconic skyscrapers and bustling streets, might not be the first place that comes to mind when you think of outdoor activities and green spaces. However, the city offers a surprising wealth of parks and outdoor experiences for both locals and visitors to enjoy. Here's a glimpse into the lush green side of the Big Apple:

Central Park: No visit to New York City is complete without a trip to Central Park. This sprawling oasis in the heart of Manhattan spans 843 acres, offering a haven of natural beauty amidst the urban jungle. Stroll along tree-lined pathways, rent a rowboat on the lake, visit the Central Park Zoo, or simply find a quiet spot to relax. In every season, Central Park offers a different charm, from vibrant foliage in the fall to outdoor concerts in the summer.

The High Line: This innovative urban park is a repurposed elevated railway line transformed into a green space with walking paths, gardens, and art installations. The High Line offers a unique perspective of the city, allowing you to meander above the streets and enjoy views of architecture and nature blending seamlessly.

Prospect Park: Located in Brooklyn, Prospect Park is a hidden gem that rivals Central Park in beauty and diversity. It features a lake, walking and biking paths, the Prospect Park Zoo, and even a botanical garden. The park often hosts events and concerts, making it a vibrant hub of activity.

Brooklyn Bridge Park: Nestled along the East River, this waterfront park boasts stunning views of the Manhattan skyline and the Brooklyn Bridge. You can play beach volleyball, kayak, or simply relax on the grassy lawns. Pier 5 is a popular spot for families, offering playgrounds and sports courts.

Governors Island: A short ferry ride from Lower Manhattan transports you to Governors Island, a car-free oasis with acres of parkland, art installations, and historic buildings. It's the perfect place to rent a bike and explore the island's unique attractions.

Rockaway Beach: If you're looking for some beach time within the city limits, Rockaway Beach in Queens is the place to be. Enjoy the sand, surf, and the famous boardwalk, where you can savor seafood at local eateries.

Wave Hill: Located in the Bronx, Wave Hill is a serene public garden and cultural center overlooking the Hudson River. Its manicured gardens, woodland trails, and art exhibitions make it a delightful escape from the city's hustle and bustle.

Pelham Bay Park: As the largest park in New York City, Pelham Bay Park in the Bronx offers a wide range of outdoor activities. Explore its hiking trails, visit the Bartow-Pell Mansion Museum, or simply enjoy a picnic in this expansive natural retreat.

Whether you're an outdoor enthusiast, a nature lover, or just seeking a break from the city's frenetic pace, New York City's parks and outdoor spaces provide a breath of fresh air and a chance to connect with nature amidst the skyscrapers. Don't miss the opportunity to discover the green side of the city that never sleeps.

7.4 Entertainment and Broadway Shows

New York City is often referred to as the cultural epicenter of the world, and one of its most iconic attractions is the dazzling world of entertainment and Broadway shows. Whether you're a theater enthusiast or simply looking for a memorable night out, the city's entertainment scene offers something for everyone.

Broadway Extravaganza:
Broadway is synonymous with New York's theater scene. The district, located in Times Square, boasts an array of theaters showcasing some of the most spectacular productions on Earth. From timeless classics like "The Phantom of the Opera" and "Les Misérables" to newer hits like "Hamilton" and "Dear Evan Hansen," the options are limitless. Be sure to book your tickets well in advance, as these shows are incredibly popular.

Off-Broadway Gems:
Beyond the glittering lights of Broadway, Off-Broadway theaters offer an alternative theatrical experience. These smaller venues host a diverse range of productions, from experimental plays and musicals to thought-provoking dramas. Don't miss the chance to explore the Off-Broadway scene for a more intimate and avant-garde experience.

Lincoln Center for the Performing Arts:

For lovers of classical music, ballet, and opera, Lincoln Center is a cultural mecca. Home to renowned institutions like the New York Philharmonic, the Metropolitan Opera, and the New York City Ballet, this sprawling complex hosts world-class performances year-round. Check their schedule for upcoming events and secure your tickets to witness breathtaking live performances.

Comedy Clubs:
New York City is also famous for its comedy clubs, where you can catch stand-up comedians at their best. Places like the Comedy Cellar and Gotham Comedy Club have launched the careers of many comedy legends. Grab a drink and prepare to laugh the night away.

Live Music Venues:
If you're a music enthusiast, NYC has a vibrant live music scene. From historic venues like the Apollo Theater in Harlem to the Bowery Ballroom in the Lower East Side, you can enjoy live performances spanning all musical genres. Keep an eye on the concert listings to catch your favorite artists in action.

Late-Night Shows:

For a unique and quintessentially New York experience, consider attending a late-night TV show taping. Shows like "Saturday Night Live" and "The Tonight Show Starring Jimmy Fallon" offer tickets to their tapings, providing a chance to witness the magic of television production up close.

Outdoor Screenings:
In the summertime, many parks and public spaces across the city host outdoor movie screenings. Pack a picnic, bring a blanket, and enjoy a movie under the stars. Bryant Park and Brooklyn Bridge Park are two popular locations for these al fresco cinema experiences.

Whether you're an aficionado of the performing arts or just seeking a night of entertainment, New York City's vibrant and diverse entertainment options guarantee an unforgettable experience. Be sure to check show schedules, purchase tickets in advance, and immerse yourself in the rich cultural tapestry of the city that never sleeps.

Chapter 8. Cultural Experiences

8.1 Art and Theater Scene

New York City boasts a vibrant and world-renowned art and theater scene, making it a cultural mecca for enthusiasts from around the globe. Whether you're a fan of classical theater, contemporary art, or experimental performances, the city offers an array of options to satisfy your artistic cravings.

Theater

1. Broadway Extravaganza: New York City's Broadway district is synonymous with theater excellence. Catching a Broadway show is a quintessential New York experience. From iconic musicals like "The Phantom of the Opera" and "The Lion King" to thought-provoking plays like "Hamilton" and "The Humans," there's something for everyone.

2. Off-Broadway Gems: If you're looking for more intimate and experimental productions, Off-Broadway theaters deliver. These venues offer a diverse range of performances, from cutting-edge dramas to avant-garde plays, often featuring emerging talent and groundbreaking narratives.

3. Shakespeare in the Park: During the summer months, don't miss the opportunity to enjoy free performances of Shakespearean classics at the Delacorte Theater in Central Park. It's an enchanting outdoor experience that combines culture with nature.

Art Galleries and Museums

1. The Met and The MoMA: The Metropolitan Museum of Art (The Met) and the Museum of Modern Art (MoMA) are two of the world's most prestigious art institutions. The Met houses an extensive collection spanning 5,000 years, while MoMA showcases modern and contemporary masterpieces by artists like Picasso, Van Gogh, and Warhol.

2. Whitney Museum of American Art: Focusing on American art of the 20th and 21st centuries, the Whitney Museum showcases innovative works and often features exhibitions from emerging artists, providing insight into the nation's evolving artistic landscape.

3. Chelsea Gallery District: Stroll through Chelsea's gallery district, where you'll find an array of

contemporary art galleries featuring cutting-edge art installations, photography, and multimedia exhibits.

Public Art and Street Art

1. Public Art Installations: Keep an eye out for the city's ever-changing public art installations. From the famous "Charging Bull" in the Financial District to temporary art exhibits in parks and plazas, New York City's streets are a canvas for creativity.

2. Graffiti and Street Art: Explore neighborhoods like Williamsburg in Brooklyn to witness the thriving street art scene. From colorful murals to thought-provoking graffiti, these expressions of urban art are a testament to the city's creative spirit.

Cultural Events

1. NYC Film Festivals: New York hosts a variety of prestigious film festivals, including the Tribeca Film Festival and the New York Film Festival, showcasing the latest in cinema from around the world.

2. Cultural Festivals: Throughout the year, the city celebrates its rich diversity with cultural festivals, such as the West Indian American Day Carnival, Diwali on Times Square, and the Chinese New Year Parade.

3. Live Performances: Beyond theater, the city offers a diverse range of live performances, including ballet, opera, and orchestral concerts at venues like the Lincoln Center and Carnegie Hall.

Whether you're a theater aficionado, an art connoisseur, or simply seeking cultural enrichment, New York City's art and theater scene promises an enriching and unforgettable experience. Be sure to plan ahead and check for ticket availability, as these cultural treasures are often in high demand.

8.2 Music and Live Performances

New York City's vibrant music and live performance scene is as diverse as the city itself, offering something for every musical taste and artistic preference. Whether you're a fan of Broadway shows, classical concerts, jazz clubs, or indie gigs, the Big Apple has it all. Here's a glimpse into the musical and live performance experiences awaiting you in New York:

1. Broadway Shows: A trip to New York wouldn't be complete without catching a Broadway production. From timeless classics like "The Phantom of the Opera" to contemporary hits like "Hamilton," the city's theater district boasts a mesmerizing array of shows. Be sure to book tickets in advance, as these performances often sell out.

2. Off-Broadway and Off-Off-Broadway: Beyond the grandeur of Broadway, Off-Broadway and Off-Off-Broadway theaters offer intimate and experimental productions. These smaller venues showcase emerging talent and provide a more immersive experience.

3. Classical Music: For classical music aficionados, venues like Carnegie Hall and Lincoln Center are a must-visit. Enjoy performances by world-renowned orchestras, chamber ensembles, and soloists in these iconic concert halls.

4. Jazz Clubs: New York City has a rich jazz history, and it's still thriving today. Visit historic clubs like the Blue Note or the Village Vanguard for unforgettable jazz performances. You might even discover new talents in cozy, underground jazz bars scattered throughout the city.

5. Indie Music Scene: If you're into indie and alternative music, Brooklyn is the place to be. Williamsburg, in particular, boasts a thriving indie music scene with numerous venues hosting live bands and artists.

6. Outdoor Concerts: During the summer, take advantage of the city's outdoor concert series. Central Park's SummerStage, Prospect Park's Celebrate Brooklyn!, and various waterfront venues offer free or ticketed outdoor performances, allowing you to enjoy music under the stars.

7. Electronic Dance Music (EDM): New York has a burgeoning EDM scene with clubs like Output, Marquee, and Schimanski regularly hosting renowned DJs and electronic music events.

8. World Music: Immerse yourself in the world's music cultures by attending performances at venues like the Rubin Museum of Art, where you can explore music from Tibet, India, and beyond.

9. Comedy Clubs and Live Comedy: In addition to music, New York City is a comedy hub. Catch stand-up comedy at clubs like the Comedy Cellar, Gotham Comedy Club, or Upright Citizens Brigade Theatre for a night of laughter.

10. Street Performers: While wandering the city's streets, you'll encounter talented street performers showcasing their skills in various art forms, from musicians to dancers and magicians. Don't forget to tip these artists for their captivating performances.

Whether you're seeking a night of classical elegance, an unforgettable Broadway show, or an underground indie gig, New York City's music and live performance scene will leave you with lasting memories and a deep appreciation for the city's artistic diversity. Be sure to check event listings and book tickets in advance to make the most of your musical journey through the city that never sleeps.

8.3 Festivals and Events

New York City is not only a year-round tourist destination but also a city that never stops celebrating. Throughout the year, the city hosts a diverse range of festivals and events that cater to a wide array of interests. Whether you're a music enthusiast, art lover, foodie, or just someone looking to soak in the vibrant atmosphere, there's always something happening in the Big Apple. Here are some of the notable festivals and events to look out for:

1. New Year's Eve in Times Square (December 31st): The world-famous New Year's Eve Ball Drop in Times Square is an iconic event. Join thousands of revelers as they count down to midnight, accompanied by live performances and a dazzling fireworks display.

2. Macy's Thanksgiving Day Parade (Fourth Thursday in November): This beloved parade features giant character balloons, marching bands, and celebrity appearances. It's a perfect way to kick off the holiday season.

3. NYC Pride March (June): Celebrate LGBTQ+ pride during this vibrant and colorful parade. It's one of the largest Pride events in the world, promoting equality and inclusivity.

4. Tribeca Film Festival (April/May): Founded by Robert De Niro, this festival showcases a wide range of films, from independent features to documentaries. It's a hub for film enthusiasts and industry professionals.

5. Governors Ball Music Festival (Late Spring/Early Summer): Held on Randall's Island, this music festival features top-tier artists from various genres, making it a must-attend event for music lovers.

6. New York Fashion Week (February/September): Join the fashion elite during Fashion Week, where designers showcase their latest collections and set the trends for the coming seasons.

7. San Gennaro Feast (September): Little Italy hosts this vibrant Italian-American street festival with parades, live music, food vendors, and religious processions.

8. West Indian American Day Carnival (Labor Day Weekend): Brooklyn comes alive with colorful costumes, Caribbean music, and a grand parade celebrating Caribbean culture.

9. New York Comedy Festival (November): Prepare to laugh out loud with top comedians performing at various venues across the city.

10. Christmas Markets (November/December): Explore the festive holiday markets at Union Square, Bryant Park, and Columbus Circle, where you can shop for unique gifts and savor seasonal treats.

11. Chinese New Year Parade (January/February): Celebrate the Lunar New Year in Chinatown with

dragon and lion dances, cultural performances, and delicious Chinese cuisine.

12. TCS New York City Marathon (First Sunday in November): Join or cheer on thousands of runners as they conquer the iconic 26.2-mile course through the city's five boroughs.

These are just a taste of the many festivals and events that New York City hosts throughout the year. Be sure to check the dates and plan your visit accordingly to immerse yourself in the city's vibrant cultural scene. Whether you're into music, arts, or simply soaking up the atmosphere, there's something for everyone in the city that never sleeps.

8.4 Historical Sites and Landmarks

New York City is a treasure trove of history, with a wealth of iconic landmarks and historical sites that have played pivotal roles in the nation's development. Explore the rich tapestry of the past as you visit these fascinating locations:

1. Statue of Liberty and Ellis Island
   - The Statue of Liberty, gifted by France in 1886, stands as a symbol of freedom and democracy. Take a ferry to Liberty Island and explore the museum inside the pedestal. Nearby, Ellis Island was the

gateway for millions of immigrants to the United States. The Ellis Island National Museum of Immigration offers a moving look at their experiences.

2. Independence Hall
  - Although not in New York City, Independence Hall in nearby Philadelphia is a must-visit for history enthusiasts. This is where the Declaration of Independence and the U.S. Constitution were debated and adopted.

3. Federal Hall
  - Located on Wall Street, Federal Hall is where George Washington took the oath of office as the first President of the United States in 1789. It's a site of great historical significance.

4. Trinity Church
  - Dating back to 1697, Trinity Church is one of the oldest churches in New York City. Visit its cemetery to see the final resting place of many notable figures from American history.

5. New York Historical Society
  - This museum offers a deep dive into the city's past through its extensive collection of artifacts,

documents, and artwork. It's a treasure trove for anyone interested in the history of New York.

6. Fraunces Tavern Museum
   - Located in Lower Manhattan, this historic tavern once served as a meeting place for revolutionaries, including George Washington. Today, it's a museum showcasing Revolutionary War artifacts and American history.

7. St. Paul's Chapel
   - This church, dating back to 1766, miraculously survived the destruction of the nearby World Trade Center towers on September 11, 2001. It serves as a poignant reminder of that tragic day.

8. Hamilton Grange National Memorial
   - Visit the former home of Alexander Hamilton, one of the Founding Fathers, and explore the museum dedicated to his life and contributions to the nation.

9. Theodore Roosevelt Birthplace National Historic Site
   - Step back in time to the early 20th century and discover the childhood home of the 26th President of the United States, Theodore Roosevelt. The site

offers a glimpse into his life and the era in which he lived.

10. General Grant National Memorial
   - Also known as Grant's Tomb, this mausoleum houses the remains of Ulysses S. Grant, the Civil War general and 18th President of the United States. It's a beautiful memorial in Riverside Park.

Exploring these historical sites and landmarks in New York City will not only deepen your understanding of the city's past but also provide a profound appreciation for the role it has played in shaping the history of the United States.

Chapter 9. Shopping in NYC

9.1 High-End Boutiques

New York City is renowned for its fashion-forward culture and status as a global fashion capital. The city's streets are lined with high-end boutiques that cater to those with a taste for luxury and style. If you're a fashion enthusiast or simply looking to indulge in some upscale retail therapy, here's a glimpse into the world of high-end boutiques in the Big Apple.

1. Fifth Avenue: Known as the "Fifth Avenue Mile of Style," this iconic street boasts a plethora of luxury boutiques. Flagship stores of renowned brands like Tiffany & Co., Saks Fifth Avenue, and Bergdorf Goodman can be found here. Whether you're shopping for fine jewelry, designer clothing, or accessories, this avenue is a must-visit for upscale shopping.

2. Madison Avenue: Located on the Upper East Side, Madison Avenue is synonymous with luxury shopping. It's home to upscale boutiques like Chanel, Prada, and Gucci. The charming streets are perfect for strolling and exploring the latest fashion trends.

3. Soho: This trendy neighborhood in lower Manhattan offers a mix of high-end boutiques alongside art galleries and cafes. You can find unique designer boutiques like Dior, Balenciaga, and Saint Laurent. Soho's cobblestone streets and historic architecture add to the shopping experience.

4. Meatpacking District: Known for its chic and upscale boutiques, the Meatpacking District is a fashionable destination. Here, you'll discover boutiques like Alexander McQueen and Diane von Furstenberg. It's also a great place for upscale dining and nightlife.

5. The Shops at Hudson Yards: Hudson Yards is a modern and innovative shopping destination on Manhattan's West Side. It's home to The Shops, a collection of high-end boutiques, including Neiman Marcus, Fendi, and Cartier. The Vessel, a stunning architectural centerpiece, adds to the allure of this area.

6. Brooklyn's Williamsburg: While Manhattan is the epicenter of luxury shopping, don't overlook Brooklyn's Williamsburg neighborhood. It offers a more eclectic and artisanal approach to fashion.

Boutiques like Bird and Catbird showcase local designers and unique pieces.

7. Boutique Hotels: Some boutique hotels in New York City have their own exclusive boutiques, such as The Greenwich Hotel in Tribeca. These boutique shops often curate a selection of designer clothing, accessories, and beauty products.

8. Sample Sales: Keep an eye out for sample sales happening throughout the city. These events offer a chance to snag high-end fashion at discounted prices. Brands often announce these sales on their websites or social media channels.

Remember that high-end boutiques in New York City cater to a variety of tastes and budgets, so you can find a wide range of fashion, from cutting-edge designs to classic luxury pieces. Exploring these boutiques isn't just about shopping; it's also an opportunity to immerse yourself in the city's fashion culture and admire the artistry that defines the New York style scene. Whether you're looking to make a statement with your wardrobe or simply window shopping, the high-end boutiques in New York City offer an unforgettable experience for fashion enthusiasts.

9.2 Thrift Stores and Markets

New York City is a fashion mecca, known for its high-end boutiques and designer stores. However, it's also a treasure trove for thrift store enthusiasts and bargain hunters. Exploring the thrift stores and markets in the city not only allows you to score unique and affordable finds but also offers a glimpse into the diverse and eclectic style of New Yorkers. Here's a guide to some of the best thrift stores and markets in New York:

1. Housing Works Thrift Shops: With various locations across the city, Housing Works is a must-visit for those seeking designer fashion, vintage clothing, and home decor. What sets them apart is that all proceeds go toward supporting individuals affected by HIV/AIDS. You can shop guilt-free and discover hidden gems.

2. Beacon's Closet: A Brooklyn favorite, Beacon's Closet offers a curated selection of secondhand clothing and accessories. They are known for their trendy and unique pieces, making it an ideal spot for fashion-forward shoppers.

3. Goodwill: Goodwill has several branches throughout NYC, providing a wide range of clothing, furniture, and household items at

budget-friendly prices. It's a reliable option for those looking for essentials without breaking the bank.

4. Vintage Markets: Beyond thrift stores, New York City hosts various vintage markets and pop-up shops. The Brooklyn Flea Market and Chelsea Market are famous for their vintage sections, offering everything from vintage clothing to antique furniture and collectibles.

5. Flea Markets and Street Fairs: The city is home to numerous flea markets and street fairs, each with its own unique charm. The Hell's Kitchen Flea Market and the Grand Bazaar NYC are great places to browse for vintage items, crafts, and artisanal goods.

6. Williamsburg, Brooklyn: If you're a fan of vintage fashion, head to Williamsburg in Brooklyn. This neighborhood is a hotspot for thrift stores and vintage boutiques, including Buffalo Exchange and Monk Vintage.

7. Astoria, Queens: Explore the thrift stores in Astoria, Queens, for a more local and less crowded shopping experience. Here, you'll find unique items and retro treasures.

8. Greenmarkets: For those interested in fresh produce, handmade crafts, and locally sourced goods, the Greenmarkets throughout the city are a delightful option. The Union Square Greenmarket is particularly famous and offers a vibrant shopping experience.

9. Secondhand Designer Shops: If you're on the hunt for luxury brands at discounted prices, consider visiting secondhand designer shops like INA, where you can find pre-owned designer clothing, handbags, and accessories.

10. Thrift Store Tours: Some companies offer guided thrift store tours, helping you navigate the city's thrift scene and discover hidden gems with the guidance of a local expert.

Whether you're a vintage fashion enthusiast, a collector of unique items, or simply looking for budget-friendly shopping options, New York City's thrift stores and markets offer something for everyone. Don't forget to explore the city's diverse neighborhoods, as each one has its own distinct thrift shopping experience waiting to be uncovered.

9.3 *Souvenirs and Unique Finds*

No trip to New York City is complete without bringing home a piece of the vibrant and diverse culture that defines this iconic metropolis. The city offers a treasure trove of souvenirs and unique finds that reflect its rich history, artistry, and contemporary trends. Here's a guide to discovering the perfect mementos to commemorate your New York experience.

1. I Love NY Merchandise: The classic "I Love NY" logo is synonymous with the city itself. You can find it on everything from t-shirts and mugs to keychains and hats. These items are quintessential New York souvenirs and make for great gifts for friends and family.

2. Broadway Memorabilia: If you're a fan of the theater, consider picking up memorabilia from a Broadway show you attend. Autographed posters, playbills, and cast recordings are cherished keepsakes that capture the magic of live performances.

3. Artisanal Foods: New York is a food lover's paradise, and you can bring some of its flavors home with you. Look for local products like bagels, artisanal chocolates, hot sauces, and craft beers.

These edible souvenirs are a delicious way to remember your trip.

4. Vintage and Antiques: Scour the vintage shops and antique stores in neighborhoods like Chelsea, Williamsburg, and the East Village. You might stumble upon unique items like vintage clothing, retro furniture, or old New York City memorabilia.

5. Jewelry and Accessories: New York City boasts numerous boutiques and markets featuring handcrafted jewelry and accessories. Whether it's a locally designed necklace, a hand-stitched leather bag, or one-of-a-kind handmade scarves, you'll find stylish and unique items.

6. Street Art Prints: The city's vibrant street art scene is renowned worldwide. Many artists offer prints of their work, making it possible to bring home a piece of the city's urban art culture. Look for pieces in galleries or from street vendors.

7. Vinyl Records: Vinyl enthusiasts will appreciate New York's thriving record stores. You can find rare and classic albums, making it an excellent place to expand your music collection.

8. Custom Souvenirs: Some shops in NYC offer personalized souvenirs like engraved jewelry or custom-printed t-shirts. These items allow you to add a personal touch to your memento.

9. Museum Gift Shops: Don't forget to explore the gift shops at the city's world-class museums. They often feature unique art prints, books, and crafts inspired by the museum's collections.

10. Local Art and Photography: New York City has a vibrant art scene, and you can find unique pieces of artwork or photography at galleries and street fairs. These pieces capture the city's essence and can adorn your home as lasting memories.

When shopping for souvenirs and unique finds in New York, remember to explore various neighborhoods and markets to discover hidden gems. These items not only serve as reminders of your trip but also offer a glimpse into the creative spirit and cultural diversity that make New York City so special.

Chapter 10. Dining and Culinary Delights

10.1 Iconic NYC Foods

New York City is a gastronomic paradise, offering a diverse array of iconic foods that reflect the city's rich cultural tapestry. From food carts on street corners to Michelin-starred restaurants, NYC has something for every palate. Here are some must-try iconic foods when visiting the Big Apple:

1. New York-style Pizza: A trip to NYC wouldn't be complete without savoring a slice of New York-style pizza. Known for its thin, foldable crust and generous toppings, you can find pizzerias on nearly every street corner. Don't miss out on classic slices, or try a creative specialty pie.

2. Bagels with Lox and Cream Cheese: NYC bagels are legendary, and there's no better way to enjoy them than with silky-smooth smoked salmon (lox) and cream cheese. This quintessential breakfast or brunch option is a staple for many New Yorkers.

3. Hot Dogs: Street vendors selling hot dogs are synonymous with New York City. Try a classic "dirty water dog" topped with mustard, onions, and sauerkraut. Alternatively, visit Gray's Papaya for

their famous "Recession Special" – two hot dogs and a drink.

4. Pretzels: Soft pretzels are a popular snack sold by vendors all over the city. These warm, doughy treats are perfect for munching while exploring iconic landmarks like Central Park or Times Square.

5. Black and White Cookies: These large, cake-like cookies with half chocolate icing and half vanilla icing are a sweet treat deeply ingrained in NYC culture. They're a delightful dessert or afternoon snack.

6. Pastrami Sandwiches: Katz's Delicatessen in the Lower East Side is renowned for its towering pastrami sandwiches. Sink your teeth into a juicy, flavorful pastrami sandwich piled high with meat and served with pickles and mustard.

7. Dim Sum in Chinatown: Head to Chinatown for a taste of authentic dim sum. Enjoy an assortment of dumplings, buns, and small plates that showcase the flavors of Chinese cuisine.

8. New York Cheesecake: Creamy, dense, and indulgent, New York-style cheesecake is a dessert

lover's dream. It's typically served plain, with fruit toppings, or drizzled with chocolate.

9. Egg Cream: Despite its name, an egg cream contains neither egg nor cream. It's a classic NYC drink made with milk, seltzer, and chocolate syrup. Head to an old-fashioned soda fountain to savor this fizzy treat.

10. Street Food: Don't hesitate to try street food vendors serving everything from falafel and gyros to tacos and arepas. These affordable and delicious options provide a taste of the city's diverse culinary offerings.

Exploring the culinary delights of New York City is an adventure in itself. Whether you're strolling through the boroughs or dining at renowned restaurants, these iconic NYC foods are sure to leave your taste buds craving more of the city's vibrant flavors.

10.2 Michelin-Star Restaurants

New York City is a gastronomic paradise, boasting a vibrant culinary scene that caters to every palate. Among its culinary treasures, the city proudly hosts numerous Michelin-starred restaurants. The Michelin Guide, renowned for its rigorous dining evaluations, awards stars to select establishments that consistently deliver exceptional dining experiences. Here's a taste of the Michelin-starred delights awaiting you in the Big Apple:

1. Per Se (3 Stars)
   - Cuisine: French-American
   - Address: 10 Columbus Cir, New York, NY 10019
   - About: Per Se, the crown jewel of Chef Thomas Keller's empire, offers a once-in-a-lifetime dining experience overlooking Central Park. Impeccable service, a nine-course tasting menu, and a breathtaking setting make this a culinary pilgrimage for food enthusiasts.

2. Eleven Madison Park (3 Stars)
   - Cuisine: Contemporary American
   - Address: 11 Madison Ave, New York, NY 10010
   - About: This world-renowned restaurant, led by Chef Daniel Humm, delivers a symphony of flavors in an art deco setting. The multi-course tasting menu showcases seasonal ingredients and is known for its innovative presentation.

3. Le Bernardin (3 Stars)
   - Cuisine: Seafood
   - Address: 155 W 51st St, New York, NY 10019

- About: Le Bernardin, under the guidance of Chef Eric Ripert, is a seafood lover's dream. The menu celebrates the finest seafood from around the world, skillfully prepared to highlight each ingredient's natural flavors.

4. Chef's Table at Brooklyn Fare (3 Stars)
  - Cuisine: Fusion
  - Address: 431 W 37th St, New York, NY 10018
  - About: Situated within an intimate kitchen setting, this culinary gem combines French and Japanese influences. A 20-course tasting menu by Chef César Ramirez showcases the finest ingredients and culinary techniques.

5. Masa (3 Stars)
  - Cuisine: Japanese
  - Address: 10 Columbus Cir, New York, NY 10019
  - About: Masa, led by Chef Masa Takayama, is a temple of Japanese cuisine. Guests experience omakase dining at its finest, where each dish is a work of art, prepared with precision and care.

6. The Modern (2 Stars)
  - Cuisine: Contemporary American
  - Address: 9 W 53rd St, New York, NY 10019
  - About: Located within the Museum of Modern Art, The Modern offers a sophisticated dining

experience. The seasonal menu showcases innovative creations in a sleek, art-filled space.

7. Jean-Georges (2 Stars)
   - Cuisine: French
   - Address: 1 Central Park W, New York, NY 10023
   - About: Renowned Chef Jean-Georges Vongerichten delivers French cuisine with a modern twist. The restaurant boasts stunning Central Park views and an extensive wine list.

Reservations are highly recommended for these Michelin-starred restaurants, as they are in high demand. Whether you're a discerning foodie or simply seeking an extraordinary culinary adventure, dining at these establishments promises an unforgettable taste of New York City's gastronomic excellence.

10.3 Budget-Friendly Eateries

New York City, often associated with high living costs, also offers a plethora of dining options that won't break the bank. From street food vendors to charming local diners, here are some budget-friendly eateries to explore during your visit:

1. Food Trucks

- New York is famous for its street food culture, with food trucks scattered across the city. Grab a delicious and affordable hot dog, falafel, or gourmet sandwich on the go. Don't miss the classic "dirty water dogs" from hot dog vendors – an NYC staple.

2. Pizza Joints
- Savor a slice of authentic New York-style pizza at local pizzerias. Places like Joe's Pizza, Di Fara Pizza, or Artichoke Basille's Pizza offer mouthwatering options at reasonable prices.

3. Ethnic Eateries
- Explore the diverse neighborhoods of NYC, and you'll find a variety of affordable international cuisine. Head to Chinatown for dumplings, Jackson Heights for Indian street food, or Sunset Park for authentic Mexican tacos.

4. Delis and Bodegas
- Delicatessens and corner bodegas serve up hearty sandwiches, salads, and breakfast options at budget-friendly prices. Order a classic bacon, egg, and cheese sandwich or a towering Reuben sandwich.

5. Noodle Shops

- For a satisfying and inexpensive meal, visit one of the many noodle shops in the city. Tuck into a bowl of ramen, pho, or hand-pulled noodles in flavorful broths.

6. Bagel Shops
   - Start your day with a New York-style bagel. Grab a freshly baked bagel with cream cheese, lox, or your favorite topping from local bagel shops.

7. Diners
   - NYC is home to classic diners where you can enjoy comfort food at affordable prices. Pancakes, omelets, and burgers are staples on their menus.

8. Food Halls
   - Food halls like Chelsea Market and Smorgasburg offer a wide array of budget-friendly culinary options. Sample dishes from different vendors, and you're sure to find something delicious without breaking the bank.

9. Slice of Pie
   - For dessert, indulge in a slice of pie from iconic spots like the Little Pie Company or Two Little Red Hens. It's a sweet way to end your meal without spending too much.

10. Happy Hour Deals
   - Many bars and restaurants in NYC offer happy hour specials with discounted drinks and appetizers. Take advantage of these deals to enjoy a relaxing evening out without straining your wallet.

When exploring New York City on a budget, these eateries not only satisfy your taste buds but also provide a taste of the city's diverse culinary landscape without emptying your pockets. Enjoy the flavors of the Big Apple while keeping your expenses in check.

10.4 Dietary Restrictions and Preferences

New York City, with its diverse culinary landscape, is a haven for food enthusiasts of all preferences and dietary restrictions. Whether you're a vegan, vegetarian, gluten-free, or have other dietary preferences, you'll find a wealth of options to satisfy your cravings. Here's a guide to navigating the city's food scene while accommodating dietary restrictions and preferences:

1. Vegan and Vegetarian Delights
   - NYC boasts a thriving vegan and vegetarian scene, with numerous dedicated eateries. Visit places like "By Chloe," "Peacefood Cafe," and "Dirt

Candy" for creative and delicious plant-based dishes.
   - Most mainstream restaurants also offer vegan and vegetarian options, so don't hesitate to ask your server for recommendations or substitutions.

2. Gluten-Free Options
   - Gluten-free dining has become increasingly accessible in NYC. Look for certified gluten-free restaurants like "Senza Gluten" or "Bistango."
   - Many pizza places now offer gluten-free crusts, and you can find gluten-free pasta in Italian restaurants.

3. Halal and Kosher Food
   - New York City is known for its diverse neighborhoods, making it easy to find authentic Halal and Kosher cuisine. Areas like Jackson Heights and Midwood are great for exploring these culinary traditions.
   - Renowned spots like "Mamouns Falafel" and "2nd Ave Deli" serve up delicious Halal and Kosher options, respectively.

4. Food Allergies
   - When dining out with food allergies, communicate your requirements clearly to the restaurant staff. Many establishments take food

allergies seriously and will accommodate your needs.
   - Check online resources and apps that list allergy-friendly restaurants and menus, making it easier to find safe options.

5. International Cuisine
   - New York's international food scene ensures there's something for every palate. From Ethiopian injera to Indian dosas, you can explore diverse global cuisines while adhering to your dietary preferences.
   - Consider neighborhoods like Flushing for incredible Asian cuisine or Little Italy for classic Italian dishes.

6. Farm-to-Table and Organic Dining
   - If you prefer organic and sustainably sourced foods, you're in luck. NYC has a growing farm-to-table movement, with restaurants like "Blue Hill" and "Gramercy Tavern" leading the way.
   - Visit local farmers' markets and specialty stores to find organic produce and products for self-catering.

7. Allergen-Friendly Groceries
   - Stock up on allergen-friendly groceries at health food stores like "Whole Foods Market" or specialty

shops like "Erin McKenna's Bakery" for gluten-free and vegan treats.

8. Dietary Apps and Resources
   - Utilize mobile apps and websites that cater to dietary restrictions, such as "Find Me Gluten Free" or "HappyCow" for vegan and vegetarian options. These resources can help you discover new dining spots.

Remember that while NYC offers a wide array of options for dietary preferences and restrictions, it's always a good practice to inform restaurants about your needs in advance to ensure a safe and enjoyable dining experience. With its culinary diversity and accommodating establishments, New York City ensures that every food lover can savor the city's flavors without compromise.

Chapter 11. Nightlife and Entertainment

11.1 Bars and Clubs

New York City's nightlife is as diverse and vibrant as the city itself. Whether you're looking for a trendy rooftop bar with breathtaking views, a historic speakeasy, a lively dance club, or a cozy neighborhood pub, the city that never sleeps has it all. Here's a glimpse into the dynamic world of bars and clubs in New York:

1. Rooftop Bars: One of the quintessential New York experiences is sipping cocktails while taking in the city's iconic skyline. Rooftop bars like "230 Fifth" and "The Press Lounge" offer spectacular views of landmarks like the Empire State Building and the Hudson River.

2. Speakeasies: Step back in time to the Prohibition era by visiting one of New York's hidden speakeasies. Places like "Please Don't Tell (PDT)" and "The Back Room" provide an intimate atmosphere, inventive cocktails, and a sense of nostalgia.

3. Dance Clubs: For those looking to dance the night away, New York offers a myriad of dance clubs, each with its unique vibe. "Output" in

Brooklyn and "Marquee" in Manhattan are renowned for their electrifying DJ sets and high-energy crowds.

4. Jazz Clubs: New York City is a jazz lover's paradise, with legendary venues like "Blue Note" and "Village Vanguard" hosting world-class jazz musicians. Enjoy soulful performances in an intimate setting.

5. Historic Pubs: Explore the city's history by visiting classic pubs like "McSorley's Old Ale House" and "The Ear Inn." These establishments have been serving patrons for over a century and offer a taste of old New York.

6. LGBTQ+ Bars: The LGBTQ+ community has a strong presence in NYC, and the city boasts a vibrant LGBTQ+ bar scene. "Stonewall Inn" in the West Village is a historic landmark that played a pivotal role in LGBTQ+ rights.

7. Brooklyn's Hip Scene: Brooklyn has carved out its own niche in the nightlife scene with a plethora of bars and clubs. Williamsburg, in particular, is known for its trendy bars like "Brooklyn Brewery" and "Output."

8. Comedy Clubs: If you're in the mood for laughter, NYC has world-famous comedy clubs like "Comedy Cellar" and "Carolines on Broadway" where you can catch top comedians.

9. Craft Beer Bars: Beer enthusiasts can explore the city's thriving craft beer scene. Brewpubs like "Other Half Brewing Company" and "Threes Brewing" offer a diverse range of locally brewed beers.

10. Karaoke Bars: Sing your heart out at New York's karaoke bars, like "Karaoke Boho" in the East Village, where you can unleash your inner rock star in private rooms.

Remember that New York City's nightlife is ever-evolving, with new spots constantly emerging. It's essential to check for current opening hours and reservations before heading out for a night on the town. Whether you're seeking a sophisticated cocktail, live music, or a wild dance floor, New York City's bars and clubs cater to every taste and mood, ensuring you'll find the perfect place to create lasting memories during your visit.

11.2 Live Music Venues

New York City is a global epicenter for culture and entertainment, and its live music scene is no exception. Whether you're a fan of jazz, rock, hip-hop, or any other genre, you'll find an abundance of live music venues catering to every taste. Here are some iconic venues that should be on any music lover's list:

1. The Apollo Theater
   Location: Harlem, Manhattan
   The historic Apollo Theater is legendary for its role in launching the careers of countless African American artists, including Ella Fitzgerald and James Brown. It's the place to experience the rich heritage of jazz, soul, and R&B.

2. Radio City Music Hall
   Location: Midtown Manhattan
   Known for its stunning Art Deco architecture, Radio City Music Hall hosts a variety of events, including live concerts by renowned artists. It's an iconic venue that offers an unforgettable experience.

3. The Bowery Ballroom
   Location: Lower East Side, Manhattan

This intimate venue has been a staple of New York's indie music scene for decades. It's a great place to catch emerging bands and established artists in an up-close setting.

4. Brooklyn Steel
   Location: Williamsburg, Brooklyn
   Located in the heart of Brooklyn, this spacious venue hosts both indie and mainstream acts. Its industrial-chic design and excellent sound system make it a top choice for live music enthusiasts.

5. Blue Note Jazz Club
   Location: Greenwich Village, Manhattan
   For jazz aficionados, the Blue Note is a must-visit. This intimate club has hosted jazz legends like Miles Davis and Herbie Hancock. Enjoy world-class jazz in a cozy setting.

6. Barclays Center
   Location: Brooklyn
   This massive arena is a hub for major concerts and sporting events. It's where you can see global superstars perform in front of thousands of enthusiastic fans.

7. The Village Vanguard
   Location: Greenwich Village, Manhattan

Steeped in history, this basement jazz club is one of the most iconic in the world. The Village Vanguard has been the stage for jazz greats like John Coltrane and Bill Evans.

8. Terminal 5

Location: Hell's Kitchen, Manhattan

Terminal 5 is a versatile venue that hosts a wide range of music acts, from electronic dance music DJs to alternative rock bands. Its multi-level layout offers diverse viewing options.

9. Webster Hall

Location: East Village, Manhattan

A historic venue with a vibrant past, Webster Hall has been a staple of the city's music scene for over a century. It hosts concerts, dance parties, and more.

10. Dizzy's Club Coca-Cola

Location: Columbus Circle, Manhattan

Located in Jazz at Lincoln Center, this jazz club offers not only exceptional music but also stunning views of Central Park. It's a sophisticated yet welcoming spot for jazz enthusiasts.

No matter which neighborhood you explore in New York City, you're likely to stumble upon a live music venue that suits your musical preferences. From intimate jazz clubs to grand arenas, the city's live music scene is as diverse and vibrant as the city itself. Be sure to check the event schedules and book your tickets in advance to ensure you don't miss out on the musical magic of the Big Apple.

11.3 Comedy Clubs and Theaters

New York City is renowned for its vibrant arts and entertainment scene, and this includes a thriving comedy and theater community. Whether you're seeking laughter or drama, the city offers an array of comedy clubs and theaters to cater to all tastes and senses of humor. Here's a glimpse into the comedy and theater scene in the Big Apple:

Comedy Clubs:

1. Comedy Cellar: Located in Greenwich Village, Comedy Cellar is a legendary venue known for hosting top-notch stand-up comedians. The intimate setting makes it a favorite spot for both locals and tourists. You might even catch surprise appearances by famous comedians working on new material.

2. The Stand: This trendy comedy club in Gramercy features a mix of established comedians and rising stars. With a sleek, modern interior and a diverse

lineup, it's a fantastic place to enjoy a night of laughter.

3. Carolines on Broadway: Situated in the heart of Times Square, Carolines is a premier comedy club known for hosting some of the biggest names in comedy. They offer a mix of headlining acts and open-mic nights.

4. Upright Citizens Brigade Theatre (UCB): UCB is famous for launching the careers of many comedy greats. They offer improv, sketch, and stand-up comedy shows. The UCB theaters are located in both Chelsea and the East Village.

Theaters:

1. Broadway: When it comes to theater, there's nothing quite like Broadway. The Theater District in Times Square boasts a dazzling array of productions, from long-running classics like "The Phantom of the Opera" to contemporary hits like "Hamilton." Be sure to book your tickets in advance, as Broadway shows are in high demand.

2. Off-Broadway: For a more intimate and often experimental theater experience, explore Off-Broadway venues. These theaters host a wide

range of productions, including edgy dramas, innovative musicals, and thought-provoking plays.

3. Lincoln Center: Home to the Metropolitan Opera, the New York City Ballet, and the New York Philharmonic, Lincoln Center is a cultural epicenter. Catching a performance here is a must for anyone with an appreciation for the performing arts.

4. Public Theater: Located in the East Village, the Public Theater is known for producing groundbreaking works and fostering emerging talent. It's the birthplace of the acclaimed musical "Hamilton."

When planning your visit to New York City, be sure to check the schedules of these comedy clubs and theaters in advance and consider making reservations. Whether you're in the mood for a night of laughter or a captivating theater performance, New York City's comedy and theater scene will undoubtedly leave you entertained and inspired.

Chapter 12. Outdoor Adventures

12.1 Central Park Activities

Central Park, often referred to as the "lungs of the city," is a sprawling oasis of greenery amidst the urban jungle of New York City. Spanning 843 acres in the heart of Manhattan, this iconic park offers a diverse range of activities and attractions for visitors of all ages and interests. Here are some of the top activities you can enjoy in Central Park:

1. Stroll and Relax: One of the simplest yet most enjoyable activities in Central Park is to take a leisurely stroll. Whether you're walking along the tree-lined pathways, lounging on the Great Lawn, or finding a quiet spot by one of the lakes, the park provides ample opportunities to unwind and soak in the natural beauty.

2. Boating: Central Park features several picturesque bodies of water, including the Central Park Lake and The Pond. Rent a rowboat or a pedalboat and take a tranquil ride while enjoying stunning views of the park's bridges and skyline.

3. Visit the Central Park Zoo: Ideal for families, the Central Park Zoo is home to a wide variety of animals, from penguins to red pandas. Kids will

love the Tisch Children's Zoo, where they can interact with farm animals.

4. Picnicking: Central Park is a perfect place for a picnic. Pick up some gourmet treats from a nearby deli or café, spread out a blanket, and savor your meal amidst the park's lush greenery.

5. Horse-Drawn Carriage Rides: For a touch of romance or a nostalgic experience, consider taking a horse-drawn carriage ride through Central Park. It's a unique way to explore the park's beauty.

6. Conservatory Garden: Discover the elegance of the six-acre Conservatory Garden, divided into three distinct styles: Italian, French, and English. It's a peaceful place to admire seasonal blooms and well-maintained landscapes.

7. Outdoor Performances: Throughout the year, Central Park hosts numerous outdoor concerts and performances. Check the schedule for events at the iconic Delacorte Theater, where Shakespeare in the Park productions are held.

8. Bethesda Terrace and Fountain: A centerpiece of the park, Bethesda Terrace is a beautiful architectural marvel. Don't forget to make a wish at

the Angel of the Waters fountain. It's a popular spot for photos.

9. Playgrounds: Central Park boasts several playgrounds designed for kids of all ages. The Heckscher Playground, in particular, is a favorite among families.

10. Sports and Recreation: From baseball fields and basketball courts to running and cycling paths, Central Park offers a wide array of recreational opportunities. You can also enjoy a game of chess or checkers at the Chess & Checkers House.

11. Central Park Conservancy Tours: To gain deeper insights into the park's history and hidden gems, consider joining a guided tour offered by the Central Park Conservancy. They offer themed tours focusing on various aspects of the park.

12. Ice Skating: In the winter, lace up your skates and glide across Wollman Rink or the Lasker Rink, two popular ice skating venues within the park.

Central Park is not just a green space but a vibrant hub of culture and recreation in the heart of Manhattan. Whether you're looking for relaxation, adventure, or cultural experiences, you'll find it all within the enchanting confines of Central Park.

12.2 Biking and Hiking Trails

New York may be renowned for its bustling cityscape, but it also offers a wealth of natural beauty and outdoor adventure opportunities. From serene hikes in lush forests to exhilarating bike rides along scenic routes, the state of New York has something to offer outdoor enthusiasts of all skill levels. Here's a glimpse into some of the best biking and hiking trails you can explore in and around New York:

Biking Trails:

1. **Hudson River Greenway:** This iconic Manhattan bike path stretches for nearly 12 miles, offering cyclists a breathtaking view of the Hudson River, the Statue of Liberty, and the city skyline. It's a perfect route for a leisurely ride, with designated lanes for cyclists.

2. **Central Park Bike Loop:** Explore the heart of Manhattan by biking around Central Park. The 6.1-mile loop takes you through the park's lush landscapes, scenic bridges, and iconic landmarks,

providing a refreshing escape from the city's hustle and bustle.

3. Governors Island: Take a ferry to Governors Island, where you'll find car-free roads and beautiful vistas. Rent a bike and explore the island's historic forts, art installations, and stunning views of Lower Manhattan.

4. North County Trailway: Located just outside New York City, this 22-mile trail runs along the former Putnam Division of the New York Central Railroad. It's a fantastic option for a longer ride through suburban and wooded areas.

Hiking Trails:

1. Adirondack High Peaks: For avid hikers, the Adirondack High Peaks region offers numerous challenging trails. Mount Marcy, the highest peak in New York, is a popular choice. Be prepared for rugged terrain and spectacular vistas.

2. Catskill Mountains: The Catskills are a hiker's paradise, with trails suitable for all levels. Consider hiking the Kaaterskill Falls Trail for a rewarding waterfall view, or tackle more challenging hikes in the Devil's Path range.

3. The Appalachian Trail: A segment of the famous Appalachian Trail runs through New York. Hike along the trail in the Hudson Valley region and enjoy diverse landscapes, from dense forests to open meadows.

4. Bear Mountain State Park: Just a short drive from the city, this park offers a range of hiking options. The popular hike to the summit of Bear Mountain provides panoramic views of the Hudson River.

5. Letchworth State Park: Known as the "Grand Canyon of the East," Letchworth State Park boasts numerous hiking trails that lead you to viewpoints overlooking dramatic waterfalls and the Genesee River Gorge.

Whether you prefer the thrill of cycling through city streets or the tranquility of hiking in the wilderness, New York has a trail for you. Make sure to check trail conditions, obtain any necessary permits, and be mindful of seasonal variations in weather when planning your outdoor adventures in the Empire State.

12.3 Waterfront Activities

New York City's iconic skyline is complemented by its stunning waterfront areas, offering a plethora of activities for visitors to enjoy. Whether you're seeking relaxation, recreation, or simply a picturesque view of the city, the city's waterfront has something for everyone.

1. Staten Island Ferry: Begin your waterfront adventure with a free ride on the Staten Island Ferry. Not only does it provide unbeatable views of the Statue of Liberty and Ellis Island, but it's also an excellent way to experience the grandeur of Manhattan's skyline.

2. Hudson River Park: Stretching for five miles along the Hudson River, Hudson River Park is a green oasis in the heart of the city. Stroll or bike along the riverfront esplanade, enjoy public art installations, and make use of recreational facilities like sports fields, tennis courts, and skate parks.

3. Brooklyn Bridge Park: Located beneath the iconic Brooklyn Bridge, this park boasts breathtaking views of the Manhattan skyline. Enjoy picnics, take a ride on Jane's Carousel, or try kayaking in the calm waters of the East River.

4. Governors Island: This former military base has been transformed into a peaceful haven. Accessible by ferry, Governors Island offers biking, picnicking, art installations, and even glamping during the summer months.

5. Circle Line Sightseeing Cruises: For a unique perspective of NYC's waterfront, consider taking a Circle Line Sightseeing Cruise. Choose from various themed tours, including the famous "Best of NYC" cruise, which circumnavigates Manhattan and offers unparalleled views.

6. The High Line: While not directly waterfront, this elevated park offers glimpses of the Hudson River and a refreshing urban green space experience. Walk amidst wildflowers, art installations, and historic railway tracks converted into walking paths.

7. Waterfront Dining: Savor the city's culinary delights at waterfront restaurants. From the seafood joints at South Street Seaport to upscale dining along the West Side Highway, there's no shortage of waterfront dining options to suit all tastes.

8. Kayaking and Paddleboarding: Many waterfront parks and locations offer kayak and paddleboard rentals. Explore the rivers and harbors at your own pace, or join a guided tour for a more immersive experience.

9. Fishing: Anglers can cast their lines in the city too. Numerous fishing spots dot the waterfront, including piers along the Hudson River and spots in Jamaica Bay, offering opportunities to reel in striped bass, flounder, and more.

10. Beach Escapes: While NYC's beaches may not be as famous as its skyscrapers, they're perfect for a summer escape. Visit Rockaway Beach in Queens or Coney Island in Brooklyn for sun, surf, and boardwalk entertainment.

New York City's waterfront activities provide a delightful contrast to the urban hustle and bustle. Whether you're seeking relaxation, adventure, or simply a scenic view, the city's waterfront areas offer a diverse range of experiences for visitors to enjoy. So, don't forget to include some waterfront exploration in your NYC itinerary!

Chapter 13. Practical Information

13.1 Local Transportation

New York City boasts an extensive and efficient local transportation system that makes exploring the city a breeze. From iconic yellow taxis to the sprawling subway network, here's a guide to getting around in the city that never sleeps:

1. Subway: The New York City subway system is one of the largest and busiest in the world, with 24/7 service. It's the most cost-effective way to travel within the city, and it connects you to almost every neighborhood. Be sure to grab a MetroCard, which can be easily refilled, for your rides.

2. Buses: NYC's bus network complements the subway system, reaching areas that may not be subway-accessible. Buses run 24/7, and you can also use your MetroCard to pay for rides. Keep in mind that bus schedules can vary due to traffic, so plan accordingly.

3. Taxis: Iconic yellow taxis are a common sight in New York City. They are readily available and can be hailed on the street. However, they tend to be more expensive than public transportation. Always ensure that the taxi has a functioning meter.

4. Ride-Sharing Apps: Uber, Lyft, and other ride-sharing apps are widely used in New York City, offering convenient and comfortable transportation options. They can be a good choice for getting around, especially during late hours or when public transportation isn't as accessible.

5. Citi Bike: For the eco-conscious traveler, New York City has a bike-sharing program called Citi Bike. You can rent bikes from various docking stations around the city and explore at your own pace.

6. Ferries: NYC's waterways are also part of the local transportation network. The Staten Island Ferry offers fantastic views of the Statue of Liberty, and other ferries can take you to destinations like Governors Island and Brooklyn's waterfront.

7. Walking: Don't underestimate the pleasure of exploring New York City on foot. Many neighborhoods are pedestrian-friendly, and walking allows you to soak in the vibrant street life, architecture, and diverse neighborhoods.

8. Accessibility: NYC's local transportation system is making strides in becoming more accessible to

people with disabilities. Many subway stations now have elevators, and buses are equipped with ramps.

9. Maps and Apps: Grab a free subway map at any station, or use smartphone apps like Google Maps, Citymapper, or Transit to plan your routes and stay updated on service changes.

10. MetroCard Tips: Pay attention to your MetroCard balance, as refilling stations are readily available. Consider getting an unlimited card if you plan to use the subway and buses frequently during your stay.

Navigating New York City's local transportation system can be an adventure in itself. Whether you choose the subway, a classic yellow cab, or a leisurely stroll through the city streets, you'll find that transportation in the Big Apple is both efficient and diverse, ensuring you can easily access all the incredible sights and experiences this vibrant metropolis has to offer.

13.2 Currency and Banking

When traveling to New York, it's essential to understand the local currency and banking system to manage your finances effectively. New York City, like the rest of the United States, uses the United

States Dollar (USD) as its official currency. Here's what you need to know about currency and banking in the Big Apple:

1. Currency Denominations: The U.S. Dollar comes in various denominations, including $1, $5, $10, $20, $50, and $100 bills, as well as coins (cents) of various values: 1 cent (penny), 5 cents (nickel), 10 cents (dime), 25 cents (quarter), and rarely used half-dollars and dollar coins.

2. Banking Facilities: New York City boasts an extensive network of banks, both local and national. Major national banks such as JPMorgan Chase, Citibank, Bank of America, and Wells Fargo have numerous branches and ATMs across the city. Additionally, you'll find various credit unions, community banks, and online banks.

3. ATMs: ATMs (Automated Teller Machines) are readily available throughout the city. You can use your debit or credit card to withdraw cash from ATMs, which are commonly found in banks, convenience stores, subway stations, and airports. Be aware that some ATMs may charge a fee for withdrawals if they are not part of your bank's network.

4. Credit and Debit Cards: Credit and debit cards are widely accepted in New York City. You can use them for most transactions, including restaurants, hotels, shopping, and attractions. Visa and MasterCard are the most commonly accepted cards, followed by American Express and Discover.

5. Currency Exchange: While credit cards are widely accepted, it's a good idea to have some cash on hand, especially for small purchases and in case you visit places that don't accept cards. Currency exchange offices can be found at major transportation hubs like airports, and some banks also offer exchange services. Be aware that exchange rates and fees may vary, so compare rates before converting currency.

6. Traveler's Checks: Traveler's checks have become less common, and many businesses no longer accept them. It's generally more convenient to use credit cards and ATMs for your financial transactions.

7. Tipping Culture: Tipping is customary in New York, and it's customary to leave a tip of 15-20% in restaurants and for services like taxi rides. Make sure to budget for tips when dining out and using services.

8. Mobile Payments: New York City has embraced mobile payment systems like Apple Pay, Google Pay, and Samsung Pay. You can use these methods at various establishments, making transactions quick and convenient.

9. Safety: New York is generally a safe place for financial transactions, but exercise caution when using ATMs at night or in less crowded areas. Shield your PIN while entering it and be aware of your surroundings.

Understanding the currency and banking system in New York City will help you navigate financial matters smoothly during your visit. Whether you prefer cards, cash, or a combination of both, you'll find that the city is well-equipped to accommodate your financial needs.

13.3 Language and Communication

New York City is a global melting pot, where cultures from around the world converge. Consequently, the city's linguistic diversity is nothing short of astonishing. While English is the primary language spoken, you'll find that numerous other languages echo through the streets. Here's what you need to know about language and communication in the Big Apple:

1. English is Widely Spoken: English is the predominant language spoken in New York City. Virtually all official communications, signs, and services are available in English. It's the primary language you'll use for everyday interactions.

2. Diverse Languages: Due to its diverse population, NYC boasts an incredible array of languages. You'll often hear Spanish, Chinese, Russian, Italian, and many other languages spoken in different neighborhoods. Many New Yorkers are bilingual or multilingual, so don't be surprised if you encounter someone who speaks several languages fluently.

3. Tourist-Friendly: New York City is a major tourist destination, so you'll find that many people in the service industry, such as hotel staff, restaurant servers, and taxi drivers, are proficient in English. They can assist tourists with directions and recommendations.

4. Multilingual Assistance: In areas with high immigrant populations, you may come across businesses and organizations that offer services in various languages. These can be particularly helpful

if you're looking for specific ethnic cuisine, cultural events, or community resources.

5. Language Apps: If you're concerned about language barriers, consider using translation apps on your smartphone. These tools can be invaluable for navigating conversations in different languages.

6. Learning Basic Phrases: While English will serve you well in most situations, learning a few basic phrases in other languages can enhance your travel experience. Locals often appreciate the effort, even if your pronunciation isn't perfect.

7. Cultural Sensitivity: In a city as diverse as New York, cultural sensitivity is essential. Embrace the rich tapestry of cultures, and always be respectful and considerate when communicating with people from different backgrounds.

8. New York Accent: New Yorkers are known for their distinctive accents and fast-paced speech. Don't be surprised if you encounter a "New York accent" – it's all part of the city's charm.

In New York City, language and communication are part of the vibrant tapestry that makes the city unique. Whether you're fluent in English or speak another language, the city's cultural diversity enriches every conversation and interaction, making your visit all the more memorable.

13.4 Health and Safety

New York City is a vibrant and exciting destination, but like any major metropolitan area, it's important for travelers to be aware of health and safety considerations to ensure a smooth and enjoyable visit. Here's a comprehensive overview of health and safety in the Big Apple:

Health Considerations:

1. Medical Facilities: New York City boasts world-class medical facilities and hospitals. In case of an emergency, dial 911 for immediate assistance. Additionally, many urgent care centers are available for non-life-threatening situations.

2. Travel Insurance: It's advisable to have comprehensive travel insurance that covers medical emergencies. Check with your insurance provider to ensure you have the appropriate coverage.

3. Pharmacies: Pharmacies, often referred to as "drugstores," are readily available throughout the

city, and you can purchase over-the-counter medications for common ailments.

4. Vaccinations: Check with your healthcare provider before traveling to ensure you have up-to-date vaccinations. Generally, there are no specific vaccinations required for New York City.

5. Tap Water: NYC tap water is safe to drink. Bottled water is available for purchase, but it's not necessary for most visitors.

Safety Tips:

1. Crime Rate: New York City has seen a significant drop in crime rates over the years. However, it's always wise to stay aware of your surroundings, especially in crowded areas, and keep an eye on your belongings.

2. Neighborhoods: While most of NYC is safe for tourists, some neighborhoods may have higher crime rates. Research your chosen area and take common-sense precautions.

3. Subway Safety: The subway system is generally safe, but travelers should be aware of their surroundings and avoid empty subway cars late at

night. Keep your belongings secure, and be cautious of pickpockets.

4. Traffic Safety: Be cautious when crossing streets, as New York City traffic can be hectic. Always use crosswalks and obey traffic signals.

5. Emergency Services: Familiarize yourself with emergency contact numbers, including 911 for immediate assistance. The NYPD (New York Police Department) is available to help with non-emergency situations as well.

6. Weather: New York experiences all four seasons, so check the weather forecast before your trip and pack accordingly. Extreme weather conditions, such as heavy snowstorms or hurricanes, are rare but possible.

Food and Dietary Considerations:

1. Food Hygiene: NYC restaurants are subject to strict health and safety regulations. Look for restaurants with good hygiene practices, and don't hesitate to ask for recommendations from locals or fellow travelers.

2. Food Allergies: If you have food allergies or dietary restrictions, inform restaurant staff, who are generally accommodating and can provide options that suit your needs.

By following these health and safety guidelines, travelers can fully enjoy the diverse and bustling atmosphere of New York City while ensuring a secure and memorable visit to this iconic destination.

Chapter 14. Day Trips and Nearby Attractions

14.1 Exploring Beyond NYC

While New York City is undoubtedly a vibrant and exciting destination, the surrounding regions offer a wealth of attractions and experiences for those willing to venture beyond the city limits. Here, we explore some captivating day trips and nearby attractions that promise to enhance your New York adventure.

1. The Hudson Valley: A Scenic Escape

Just a short drive north of New York City lies the picturesque Hudson Valley, a region renowned for its stunning landscapes, historic sites, and charming towns. Some highlights include:

- Historic Hudson: Visit this charming town, known for its antique shops, art galleries, and beautiful Hudson River views.

- Dia Beacon: Art enthusiasts will appreciate the contemporary art museum housed in a former Nabisco box-printing factory.

- Storm King Art Center: Explore vast outdoor sculptures set amidst rolling hills and woodlands, providing a unique blend of art and nature.

- Bear Mountain State Park: Enjoy hiking, picnicking, and breathtaking views from the summit of Bear Mountain.

2. Long Island: Beaches and Vineyards

A quick trip eastward brings you to Long Island, where you can bask in beautiful beaches and explore renowned vineyards:

- The Hamptons: A playground for the rich and famous, The Hamptons offers pristine beaches, upscale boutiques, and fine dining.

- North Fork Wineries: Embark on a wine-tasting tour of North Fork's wineries, producing world-class vintages in a picturesque setting.

- Montauk: Known as "The End," Montauk offers excellent surfing, lighthouse tours, and a laid-back coastal atmosphere.

3. Historic Sites in Westchester

Westchester County, just north of the city, is steeped in history:

- Sleepy Hollow: Visit the legendary town of Sleepy Hollow, home to the author Washington Irving and the famous Headless Horseman.

- Philipsburg Manor: Step back in time at this living history museum, showcasing a Dutch colonial-era farm.

- Kykuit, the Rockefeller Estate: Tour the grand mansion and gardens of the Rockefeller family, featuring impressive art collections.

4. New Jersey Gems

Across the Hudson River, New Jersey offers attractions worth exploring:

- Liberty State Park: Get panoramic views of the Statue of Liberty and Manhattan skyline, as well as visit the Liberty Science Center.

- Princeton University: Stroll through the beautiful campus and explore the historic town of Princeton.

- Grounds for Sculpture: Admire a diverse collection of contemporary sculptures set within beautifully landscaped grounds.

5. The Adirondack Mountains: Wilderness Adventure

For those seeking outdoor adventures, consider a longer day trip or weekend getaway to the Adirondack Mountains:

- Lake Placid: Known for hosting the Winter Olympics, it's a haven for outdoor enthusiasts with hiking, skiing, and beautiful lakes.

- Saratoga Springs: Explore the historic downtown, attend horse races, and relax in mineral springs.

Exploring these day trips and nearby attractions from New York City adds depth to your experience, providing a diverse range of landscapes, activities, and cultural treasures that complement the city's urban excitement. Whether you're interested in history, nature, or relaxation, these destinations offer a chance to escape the bustling metropolis and uncover the hidden gems of the surrounding region.

Chapter 15. Traveling with Pets

15.1 Pet-Friendly Accommodations

New York City, known for its bustling streets and vibrant culture, is also a welcoming destination for pet owners. If you're planning to bring your furry friend along on your trip, there are plenty of pet-friendly accommodations available. Here's a guide to some of the best options:

1. Pet-Friendly Hotels

Many hotels in New York City are pet-friendly and offer a range of amenities for your four-legged companion. Some popular choices include:

  - The Kimpton Hotel Eventi: Located in Chelsea, this luxury hotel welcomes pets of all sizes and provides pet beds, food bowls, and treats upon arrival.

  - The Standard High Line: Situated in the Meatpacking District, this trendy hotel allows pets and even offers a rooftop dog park with stunning views of the city.

  - The Benjamin: This boutique hotel in Midtown East provides a VIPaws program, complete with pet beds, food, and water bowls, and a dog-friendly concierge service.

2. Vacation Rentals

If you prefer a home-away-from-home experience, consider renting a pet-friendly vacation apartment or Airbnb. These options often offer more space and privacy for you and your pet. Just be sure to check the property's pet policy before booking.

3. Pet-Friendly Boutique Hotels

New York City is home to several boutique hotels that cater specifically to pet owners. They go the extra mile to ensure both you and your pet have a comfortable stay. Look out for places like:

  - The Marmara Park Avenue: This boutique hotel in NoMad offers pet-friendly rooms and a rooftop garden where your pet can stretch their legs.

  - The Greenwich Hotel: Located in Tribeca, this luxury hotel allows pets and provides pet beds and bowls, making your pet feel right at home.

4. Extended-Stay Options

If you plan to stay in New York for an extended period, consider pet-friendly extended-stay hotels like:

  - Element New York Times Square West: These eco-friendly suites in Times Square are not only comfortable but also welcome pets, making it suitable for longer stays.

5. Hostels and Budget-Friendly Accommodations

Traveling on a budget with your pet? Some hostels and budget-friendly hotels in New York City offer pet-friendly rooms. While the amenities may be more basic, they can be a great choice for frugal travelers.

Remember to call ahead and confirm the pet policy, any associated fees, and whether there are restrictions on pet size or breed. Additionally, be a responsible pet owner by keeping your pet on a leash in public areas, cleaning up after them, and respecting the rules of the accommodation.

With these pet-friendly accommodation options in mind, you and your furry companion can enjoy the wonders of New York City together. Whether you're exploring Central Park or strolling through the neighborhoods, your pet can be a part of the adventure in the city that never sleeps.

15.2 Dog Parks and Pet Services

New York City isn't just a bustling metropolis for humans; it's also a vibrant and pet-friendly city for your furry companions. Whether you're a local with a four-legged friend or visiting the city with your pet, there are plenty of dog parks and pet services to explore. Here's a guide to ensure your pet has a great time in the Big Apple.

Dog Parks:
1. Central Park Dog Runs: Located within Central Park, these dedicated areas provide ample space for your dog to run and play. The Central Park Conservancy operates several off-leash areas, ensuring your pet's safety while they socialize with other dogs.

2. Hudson River Park Dog Run: Enjoy stunning views of the Hudson River while your dog romps in this spacious dog run. It's a perfect spot for a game of fetch or some off-leash fun.

3. Prospect Park Dog Beach: This park in Brooklyn offers a unique experience with a designated dog

beach. Let your pup splash around in the water and cool off during the summer months.

4. Washington Square Park Dog Run: Located in the heart of Greenwich Village, this dog run provides a convenient escape for urban pet owners and their dogs. It's a great place to mingle with locals and their pets.

5. Tompkins Square Park Dog Run: Found in the East Village, this historic park offers a lively dog run where dogs can socialize and enjoy some exercise. It's known for its vibrant dog-loving community.

Pet Services:
1. Veterinary Care: New York City boasts numerous veterinary clinics and hospitals that provide top-notch care for your pets. In case of emergencies or routine check-ups, you'll find reliable services throughout the city.

2. Pet Grooming: Pamper your pet at one of the many pet grooming salons. From a basic bath to stylish haircuts, these professionals will keep your pet looking and feeling their best.

3. Pet-Friendly Accommodations: Many hotels in the city are pet-friendly, ensuring your furry companion can stay with you in comfort. Be sure to check their policies and any additional fees.

4. Pet Supply Stores: NYC offers a plethora of pet supply stores, from boutique shops to large chain stores. You can easily find everything your pet needs, from food and toys to stylish accessories.

5. Pet Sitting and Walking Services: If you plan to explore the city without your pet, numerous pet sitting and dog walking services can provide reliable care while you're away. Many professionals are experienced in handling pets of all sizes and breeds.

6. Pet-Friendly Restaurants and Cafes: Some restaurants and cafes in the city welcome pets in their outdoor seating areas. It's a great way to enjoy a meal or a cup of coffee with your furry friend by your side.

Remember to check local regulations regarding leash laws and cleanliness in public spaces to ensure a positive experience for both your pet and fellow New Yorkers. With a wealth of dog parks and pet services, New York City is a welcoming destination for pet owners and their beloved animals.

15.3 Tips for Traveling with Pets

Traveling with your beloved pets to New York City can be an enjoyable experience with some careful planning. Here are essential tips to ensure a smooth and enjoyable trip for both you and your furry companions:

1. Pet-Friendly Accommodations: Before booking your accommodation, ensure it's pet-friendly. Many hotels in New York welcome pets, and some even offer special amenities like dog beds and treats. Make reservations well in advance to secure your spot.

2. Research Pet Policies: Understand the specific pet policies of your chosen accommodation. Some hotels may have size or breed restrictions, and others may charge pet fees or deposits. Clarify these details in advance.

3. Transportation: When traveling within the city, consider pet-friendly transportation options. New York City's subway system allows small pets in carriers, while larger dogs should be leashed and well-behaved. Taxis and rideshares also

accommodate pets; just inform the driver in advance.

4. Pet Supplies: Pack all the necessary supplies, including food, water, bowls, toys, and medications. Ensure your pet is comfortable and has familiar items to ease the transition.

5. Safety First: Keep your pet's identification up to date with your current contact information. A collar with an ID tag and a microchip can help in case your pet gets lost.

6. Exploring the City: While exploring NYC, adhere to local leash laws. Be a responsible pet owner by cleaning up after your pet and disposing of waste in provided bins. Many parks in the city have designated off-leash areas where dogs can play.

7. Pet-Friendly Parks: Visit some of New York's pet-friendly parks like Central Park's designated dog areas, Tompkins Square Park, and Madison Square Park, where pets are welcome on leashes.

8. Pet Services: New York City offers various pet services, from grooming salons to veterinary clinics. Familiarize yourself with the nearest pet services in case of emergencies or routine care.

9. Pet-Friendly Dining: Some NYC restaurants with outdoor seating allow well-behaved pets to join you. Check with the restaurant in advance, and be sure your pet is comfortable in busy environments.

10. Local Pet Events: Keep an eye out for pet-related events happening during your stay. New York hosts various pet-friendly events, such as dog-friendly parades and charity walks.

11. Plan Indoor Activities: Be mindful of weather conditions. NYC can be hot in the summer and cold in the winter. Plan indoor activities like visiting pet boutiques or exploring pet-friendly museums.

12. Emergency Contact: Know the nearest 24-hour veterinary clinics and emergency pet hospitals in case of unexpected health issues.

13. Hydration: Ensure your pet stays well-hydrated, especially during hot summer months. Carry a portable water bowl and offer regular water breaks.

14. Respect Others: Not everyone is a pet lover. Be considerate of others in public spaces and accommodations, and ensure your pet's behavior is impeccable.

By following these tips, you can enjoy a memorable trip to New York City with your pets while ensuring their safety and comfort. NYC's pet-friendly atmosphere makes it an excellent destination for four-legged travelers.

Chapter 16. Resources and Contacts

16.1 Tourist Information Centers

When you're exploring the bustling streets of New York City, it's always reassuring to know that you can find reliable sources of information and assistance to enhance your travel experience. New York City boasts a network of Tourist Information Centers that are designed to make your visit more convenient and enjoyable. These centers serve as hubs of knowledge, offering a wealth of information, maps, brochures, and friendly assistance for travelers from all walks of life.

Locations
Tourist Information Centers are strategically placed throughout the city, ensuring accessibility to tourists. You can find them at key locations, including:

1. Times Square Visitor Center: Located right in the heart of Times Square, this bustling center is perfect for those exploring the Theater District, Midtown, and nearby attractions.

2. Official NYC Information Center: Nestled at the southern tip of Manhattan, near Battery Park and the Statue of Liberty ferry terminal, this center is a

great starting point for tourists heading to the Financial District or catching a boat to Liberty Island.

3. Grand Central Terminal: Conveniently situated within one of New York's most iconic transportation hubs, this information center assists travelers arriving or departing via Grand Central.

4. Brooklyn Information Center: For those exploring the vibrant borough of Brooklyn, this center is located in the popular DUMBO neighborhood, offering insights into local attractions and events.

5. Harlem Visitor Center: Discover the cultural richness of Harlem with the help of this information center, located in the historic neighborhood.

Services
At these Tourist Information Centers, you can expect a wide range of services, including:

1. Maps and Brochures: Pick up free maps and brochures that provide details about attractions, dining options, and upcoming events.

2. Friendly Staff: Knowledgeable staff members are on hand to answer your questions, provide directions, and offer recommendations tailored to your interests.

3. Multi-Lingual Assistance: New York City welcomes visitors from around the world, and many of these centers offer multi-lingual assistance to ensure everyone feels at home.

4. Ticket Sales: Some centers also facilitate the sale of tickets to popular attractions, saving you time and effort.

5. Event Information: Stay updated on the latest concerts, exhibitions, and festivals happening during your visit.

6. Accessibility Information: Inclusivity is a priority in New York City, and these centers can provide information on accessible attractions and services for travelers with disabilities.

Digital Resources
In addition to in-person assistance, most Tourist Information Centers offer digital resources, including Wi-Fi access and computer terminals where you can browse websites, make reservations,

or print tickets. You can also find official NYC tourism apps to enhance your mobile experience while exploring the city.

Whether you're a first-time visitor or a returning traveler, these Tourist Information Centers are valuable resources for making the most of your trip to the Big Apple. They exemplify New York City's commitment to ensuring that every visitor has a memorable and enriching experience in this vibrant metropolis.

16.2 Useful Websites and Apps

In the digital age, navigating the bustling streets of New York City has never been easier, thanks to a plethora of websites and apps designed to enhance your travel experience. Whether you're looking for directions, dining recommendations, or a way to navigate the city's extensive public transportation system, these digital resources can be invaluable. Here are some of the most useful websites and apps to keep handy during your trip to the Big Apple:

1. Google Maps: This widely-used mapping app is your best friend for navigating the city's intricate grid system, subway routes, and even provides real-time traffic updates. It also offers public transportation schedules and walking directions.

2. CityMapper: For those who want to master NYC's public transportation system, CityMapper is a top choice. It provides detailed transit options, including subways, buses, and even bike-sharing programs.

3. Yelp: When it comes to finding great places to eat, Yelp is a go-to app. Read user reviews, view photos, and discover the best restaurants, cafes, and bars in your area.

4. OpenTable: For securing restaurant reservations, OpenTable is a must-have app. It allows you to browse dining options, read reviews, and book a table seamlessly.

5. Time Out New York: Stay up-to-date with the latest events, concerts, theater shows, and exhibitions happening in the city. Time Out New York offers a comprehensive calendar of entertainment options.

6. Uber and Lyft: Ride-sharing services like Uber and Lyft are convenient for getting around the city, especially if you're in a hurry or traveling with a group.

7. MTA Subway Time: This official app from the Metropolitan Transportation Authority (MTA) provides real-time subway information, helping you plan your subway journeys with accuracy.

8. New York Pass: If you're planning to visit numerous attractions, consider the New York Pass app, which provides access to over 100 popular landmarks and museums with a single pass.

9. Citi Bike: New York City's bike-sharing program is an eco-friendly way to explore the city. Use the Citi Bike app to find nearby bike stations and check availability.

10. NYC.gov: The official website of the City of New York, NYC.gov, offers a wealth of information on government services, emergency alerts, and important city announcements.

11. StreetEasy: If you're looking for apartments or vacation rentals in New York, StreetEasy is a valuable resource, providing real estate listings and neighborhood information.

12. Central Park Conservancy: For a visit to Central Park, this app offers maps, guided tours, and information about park events and amenities.

13. Duolingo: If you're interested in learning some basic phrases in different languages, Duolingo can be handy for communicating with the diverse population of New York City.

These websites and apps can significantly enhance your New York City experience, making it easier to explore, dine, and enjoy all that this vibrant metropolis has to offer. Before your trip, consider downloading these digital tools to your smartphone or tablet for easy access on the go.

Chapter 17. Itinerary Ideas

17.1 One Week in NYC

New York City is a sprawling metropolis bursting with culture, history, and endless attractions. If you have the luxury of spending one week in the Big Apple, you can explore a diverse range of neighborhoods, iconic landmarks, and unique experiences. Here's a comprehensive itinerary to make the most of your week in NYC:

Day 1: Arrival and Times Square
- Morning: Arrive in NYC and check into your accommodation.
- Afternoon: Start your journey at Times Square, soak in the neon lights, and grab a bite at a nearby eatery.
- Evening: Watch a Broadway show for a quintessential New York experience.

Day 2: Lower Manhattan
- Morning: Visit the 9/11 Memorial and Museum to pay respects and learn about the tragic events of 9/11.
- Afternoon: Explore Battery Park and take a ferry to the Statue of Liberty and Ellis Island.

- Evening: Stroll through the historic streets of the Financial District and dine in one of the area's excellent restaurants.

Day 3: Museums and Central Park
- Morning: Spend your morning at the Metropolitan Museum of Art (The Met).
- Afternoon: Explore the American Museum of Natural History.
- Evening: Head to Central Park for a leisurely walk, row a boat on the lake, or attend a concert at the Central Park SummerStage.

Day 4: Midtown Manhattan
- Morning: Discover the art at the Museum of Modern Art (MoMA).
- Afternoon: Visit Rockefeller Center and take a guided tour or go ice-skating in winter.
- Evening: Enjoy a panoramic view of the city from the Top of the Rock Observation Deck.

Day 5: Upper Manhattan and Harlem
- Morning: Explore the iconic Cathedral of St. John the Divine.
- Afternoon: Visit the historic Apollo Theater in Harlem.
- Evening: Savor soul food in Harlem and experience the vibrant local music scene.

Day 6: Brooklyn Adventure
- Morning: Cross the Brooklyn Bridge on foot for stunning views of the skyline.
- Afternoon: Explore Brooklyn's neighborhoods, like DUMBO and Williamsburg.
- Evening: Catch a concert at the Barclays Center or dine at a trendy Brooklyn restaurant.

Day 7: The Bronx and Farewell
- Morning: Discover the Bronx's cultural gems, including the Bronx Museum of the Arts and the Bronx Zoo.
- Afternoon: Explore the Bronx Botanical Garden.
- Evening: Enjoy a final meal in NYC at a local favorite restaurant.

This one-week itinerary offers a diverse taste of New York City, from its famous landmarks to its vibrant neighborhoods. Of course, NYC has much more to offer, so feel free to adjust the itinerary based on your interests, and don't forget to immerse yourself in the city's unique atmosphere and energy as you explore.

17.2 Weekend Getaway Itinerary

New York City is a bustling metropolis filled with endless attractions and experiences. If you have just a weekend to explore the city, don't worry; you can still make the most of your time with this carefully crafted itinerary.

Day 1: Exploring Manhattan

Morning:
- Start your day with a classic New York breakfast at a local diner or café.
- Head to Central Park, where you can enjoy a leisurely stroll or even rent a bike to explore its vast greenery.

Lunch:
- Grab a bite at one of the many food trucks or street vendors within the park, offering a variety of delicious options.

Afternoon:
- Visit the iconic Museum of Modern Art (MoMA) to admire its world-class collection of art and exhibitions.
- Take a walk down Fifth Avenue and window shop at luxury boutiques.

Dinner:

- Experience fine dining at a restaurant in the Theater District, where you can savor a pre-theater dinner.

Evening:
- Catch a Broadway show at one of the renowned theaters in Times Square.
- Stroll around Times Square at night when it's illuminated with dazzling billboards.

Day 2: Exploring More of NYC

Morning:
- Enjoy a bagel with cream cheese or a classic New York-style deli breakfast.
- Visit the historic Statue of Liberty and Ellis Island, which you can reach by taking a ferry from Battery Park.

Lunch:
- Grab a quick bite at a local café or food market in Lower Manhattan.

Afternoon:
- Explore the 9/11 Memorial and Museum, a poignant tribute to the events of September 11, 2001.

- Walk across the Brooklyn Bridge for stunning views of the Manhattan skyline.

Dinner:
- Savor authentic Italian cuisine in the charming neighborhood of Little Italy.
- Alternatively, dine in one of the trendy restaurants in the DUMBO (Down Under the Manhattan Bridge Overpass) area of Brooklyn.

Evening:
- Take a leisurely stroll along the Brooklyn Heights Promenade, offering breathtaking views of the city.
- End your evening with a drink at a rooftop bar overlooking Manhattan.

Day 3: Cultural and Culinary Delights

Morning:
- Start your day with a hearty breakfast, perhaps trying a New York-style breakfast sandwich.
- Explore the Metropolitan Museum of Art (the Met), one of the world's largest and most prestigious art museums.

Lunch:
- Have lunch at a cozy café on the Upper East Side or enjoy a picnic in Central Park.

Afternoon:
- Visit the Guggenheim Museum, famous for its distinctive spiral architecture and modern art collections.
- Spend some time exploring the Upper West Side and its charming brownstone-lined streets.

Dinner:
- Dine at a trendy restaurant in the West Village, known for its vibrant dining scene.

Evening:
- Take a nighttime stroll through the historic West Village streets, filled with shops and cafes.
- End your weekend with a jazz or live music performance at a local jazz club.

This weekend getaway itinerary offers a taste of the diverse experiences New York City has to offer, from iconic landmarks to cultural institutions and delicious culinary adventures. Remember to book tickets for attractions in advance when possible to make the most of your short stay in the city. Enjoy your whirlwind New York adventure!

17.3 Family-Friendly Itinerary

Day 1: Exploring Midtown Manhattan

- Morning: Start your adventure at Times Square, the bustling heart of Manhattan. Let your kids soak in the dazzling lights and energy of this iconic location.

- Late Morning: Head to the Museum of Modern Art (MoMA). While the art may not be everyone's cup of tea, the impressive sculpture garden and interactive exhibits make this museum engaging for all ages.

- Lunch: Enjoy a family lunch at one of the many nearby restaurants, such as Ellen's Stardust Diner, where you can dine while talented Broadway hopefuls sing.

- Afternoon: Stroll to Rockefeller Center and take the famous NBC Studio Tour. Kids will love seeing the sets of their favorite shows.

- Evening: Catch a family-friendly Broadway show, like "The Lion King" or "Aladdin."

Day 2: Central Park and Museums

- Morning: Spend the morning in Central Park. Rent bikes or paddleboats, visit the Central Park

Zoo, and explore the charming Conservatory Garden.

- Lunch: Grab a picnic lunch from one of the nearby vendors and enjoy it by the Bethesda Terrace and Fountain.

- Afternoon: Head to the American Museum of Natural History. The dinosaur exhibits and the Hayden Planetarium are sure to captivate young minds.

- Evening: Have dinner at one of the family-friendly eateries near the museum, and then take a leisurely walk through Central Park to see the city lights.

Day 3: Exploring Lower Manhattan

- Morning: Start your day with a ferry ride to the Statue of Liberty and Ellis Island. Kids will be fascinated by the history and grandeur of these landmarks.

- Late Morning: Visit the immersive National September 11 Memorial & Museum. While solemn, it's an important experience for older children.

- Lunch: Dine at one of the family-friendly restaurants in Battery Park City.

- Afternoon: Take a leisurely stroll across the Brooklyn Bridge for breathtaking views of the skyline.

- Evening: Explore DUMBO (Down Under the Manhattan Bridge Overpass) in Brooklyn, with its artsy vibe and scenic waterfront. Grab some ice cream and let the kids play in the park.

Day 4: Cultural and Artistic Exploration

- Morning: Start your day at the Intrepid Sea, Air & Space Museum, where kids can explore a real aircraft carrier, the Space Shuttle Pavilion, and more.

- Lunch: Enjoy a meal at one of the nearby restaurants in Hell's Kitchen.

- Afternoon: Visit the Children's Museum of the Arts in the West Village, where young artists can get creative.

- Evening: Wrap up your family adventure with a visit to Serendipity 3, famous for its extravagant desserts.

This family-friendly itinerary offers a perfect blend of fun, education, and exploration, ensuring that both kids and adults have a memorable time experiencing the best of New York City together.

17.4 Romantic Couples' Itinerary

New York City, with its iconic skyline, charming neighborhoods, and a plethora of romantic experiences, is a perfect destination for couples looking to create lasting memories. Whether you're celebrating a special occasion or just want to rekindle the romance, this itinerary will guide you through a delightful journey in the city that never sleeps.

Day 1: Exploring Iconic Landmarks
- Morning: Start your day with breakfast at a cozy café in Greenwich Village.
- Late Morning: Stroll through Central Park, rent a rowboat, or enjoy a horse-drawn carriage ride.
- Lunch: Head to The Boathouse in Central Park for a romantic lakeside lunch.
- Afternoon: Visit the Top of the Rock Observation Deck for breathtaking views of the city.

- Evening: Dine at a Michelin-starred restaurant in Midtown Manhattan, followed by a Broadway show.

Day 2: Art and Culture
- Morning: Enjoy a leisurely breakfast at a French bakery in SoHo.
- Late Morning: Explore the world-famous Metropolitan Museum of Art (the Met).
- Lunch: Have a picnic in the beautiful Cloisters Museum gardens.
- Afternoon: Take a romantic walk along the High Line, an elevated park with greenery and art installations.
- Evening: Experience the magic of The Met Opera or a classical performance at Lincoln Center.

Day 3: Waterfront Romance
- Morning: Have a brunch with a view at a waterfront restaurant in DUMBO, Brooklyn.
- Late Morning: Explore the enchanting Brooklyn Botanic Garden.
- Lunch: Enjoy a food tour of Smorgasburg, a food market with diverse cuisine options.
- Afternoon: Take a scenic walk across the Brooklyn Bridge.
- Evening: Savor a candlelit dinner at a romantic restaurant in Williamsburg.

Day 4: Hidden Gems and Serenity
- Morning: Visit the charming West Village for a delightful breakfast.
- Late Morning: Explore the lesser-known gem, the Frick Collection, a mansion filled with art.
- Lunch: Dine at a cozy bistro in the West Village.
- Afternoon: Relax in the enchanting Conservatory Garden in Central Park.
- Evening: Enjoy a quiet evening with a sunset ferry ride to Staten Island for panoramic views of the Statue of Liberty.

Day 5: Culinary Delights
- Morning: Start the day with a visit to a local farmer's market for fresh ingredients.
- Cooking Class: Take a couples' cooking class and learn to prepare a romantic meal together.
- Afternoon: Enjoy your culinary creation at a scenic picnic spot in Central Park.
- Evening: Sip on cocktails at a rooftop bar overlooking the city.

This Romantic Couples' Itinerary in New York offers a mix of iconic landmarks, cultural experiences, and intimate moments, ensuring you and your partner have an unforgettable time in the city that epitomizes romance. Customize it to your preferences and enjoy your romantic getaway in the Big Apple.

The Tale of the Starry Skyline

In a time long ago, before the towering skyscrapers of New York City graced the world's horizon, there was a small village nestled on the shores of a vast and tranquil lake. This village, known as "Laketon," was a place of simplicity and serenity, where people lived harmoniously with nature.

The heart of Laketon was its beautiful lake, said to be enchanted by ancient spirits. Every night, as the sun dipped below the horizon, the people of Laketon would gather on the shores to witness a magical phenomenon. The night sky would come alive with countless stars, and among them shone a single, radiant star that was brighter and more mesmerizing than any other.

Legend had it that this star held the dreams of the village within its gleaming light. It was said that when someone from Laketon wished upon the star with a pure heart, their dreams would come true. As a result, the people of the village lived content and fulfilled lives.

However, there was one young woman named Ella who had dreams that extended beyond the boundaries of Laketon. She longed to explore the world beyond the village, to see the bustling cities she had heard of in stories. Ella's dreams were so ambitious that they seemed impossible to contain within Laketon's simple way of life.

One night, Ella stood by the lake, gazing up at the radiant star. With tears in her eyes, she made a heartfelt wish, "Star of Laketon, guide me to the world beyond, where dreams soar higher than the highest skyscraper."

The star twinkled brightly in response, and a gentle wind whispered through the village. The next morning, Ella woke up to find herself standing amidst the towering skyscrapers of New York City. She had been transported from her peaceful village to the city of dreams, and her wish had come true.

Ella embraced the city's energy, its diversity, and its relentless pursuit of dreams. She became a storyteller, sharing the tale of the Starry Skyline with people from all walks of life. And so, the legend of the star from Laketon lived on, not just as a beacon of hope for a single village but as a symbol of the boundless possibilities that await those who dare to dream.

As you explore the endless wonders of New York City, remember the tale of the Starry Skyline, and let it inspire you to chase your own dreams, no matter how high they may reach. In the city that never sleeps, dreams can become reality, just as they did for Ella, the girl who wished upon a star.

Printed in Great Britain
by Amazon